19-1

THE EUCHARIST
TODAY

THE EUCHARIST TODAY

By
H.-M. Feret, O.P.
—

Translated by
Aimée Bourneuf, R.S.C.J.

BX
2215, 2
, F4/3

PAULIST PRESS DEUS BOOKS

NEW YORK   GLEN ROCK   WESTMINSTER

TORONTO   AMSTERDAM

Contents

Contents

Foreword

The Constitution of the Liturgy promulgated by Vatican II sets the paschal mystery at the center of the economy of salvation and consequently, at the center of the liturgy of which the Eucharist is the innermost heart. The Mass, or Eucharist, is therefore essentially paschal.

In this essay, which originally appeared in the journal *Lex Orandi*, we show the Mass as our Pasch, the Pasch of Christ, and at the same time, the Pasch of all Christians. Obviously, such a theme is full of meaning for the Mass, giving it communal and cosmic signficance through its connection with salvation history.

We have here a remarkable application of that concrete and historical theology which characterized Vatican II, and was particularly appreciated by such non-Catholic observers as Professor Skydsgaard, speaking to His Holiness, Pope Paul VI, on October 17, 1963.

Introduction

Pastoral Teaching and Concrete Historical Theology

Pastoral teaching is traditionally supposed to follow as closely as possible the bible and the liturgy. Of course, the speculative aspects of theology discussed there should be known and applied by the pastor. By warning him of the problems that the truths of faith presented hitherto or still present today, theology arouses or stimulates his own curiosity about them and can direct a continual study of them. It is still true that his teaching of the faithful, a pastoral not a scholastic teaching, concerns itself directly with the truths of faith, not with theological speculation, and still less with technical discussions arising from their study. This requires a method of exposition following as closely as possible to biblical and historical sources in which these truths were revealed to the People of God. That is the basic reason, moreover, why pastoral teaching has traditionally given such importance to sacred history, which unfortunately is not the case at present.

On the concrete and historical level, that of revelation and the biblical sources that show us its progressive stages, there is a continuous development which although it stems from a logic other than the formal logic of speculative thought, is nonetheless real and enlightening. Even as there is an internal coherence among the various

3

teachings of revelation which theology should explain by relating them to some basic principles and finally to God, so among the successive moments of revelation, there is a pedagogical progression and a providential logic, centered on Jesus, the Messiah and Son of the living God. The theologian must carefully explain this logic and this progression, since they are on a deeper level than the pronouncements and doctrines; they are on the level of facts and history, of which the pronouncements and doctrines are, in a way, only the abstract expression. Since Revelation is first spelled out in history, by confining oneself wholly to the concrete and historical level of facts one is necessarily in a more immediate relation with the logical development of revelation than the subsequent conclusions of speculative theology.

When confronted with this revelation, the theologian and also the pastor, will have to discern the continuity and the progress of these divine messages. This can be done only with the help of research according to historical methods which deal with the knowledge of the interaction and evolution of things past. Thus we emphasize again the close relationship which should exist between pastoral teaching and sacred history, provided that the latter is not understood as a collection of anecdotes or tales, but as a way of manifesting the providential meaning of the history of the People of God and of discerning its characteristic phases whereby, in that history, the mysteries of God were revealed and communicated to that People.

It is basically a question of bringing out on the concrete level associated with both history and pastoral teaching what Christian antiquity called the "economy," and which is reputedly different from "theology." This is, moreover, what was done by the authors of the sacred

books, whose most extensive developments remain close
to the historical and concrete realities of the People of
God, and among whom, for example, what we would call
dogmas are formulated more often as extensions of moral
propositions rather than as necessary *a priori* conclusions. This was also done by the primitive Church in its
creeds, where the trinitarian doctrine itself is taught in
a framework of "economy" rather than "theology." This
has been done even to the present day in the sacred
liturgy. Liturgy, creeds, and the books of scripture, were
chosen by the Church and by the Holy Spirit, in order
to give the Christian community its pastoral teaching.

Such, in short, is the methodology intended by this
essay. It can already be surmised, and it will perhaps
be seen more clearly at the conclusion that we are not
merely referring to a method of exposition, and less to an
effort to popularize. This is an effort to prove by example
the importance for pastoral teaching of the primary and
positive function, if you like, of theology alone.

The Pastoral Starting Point

Since we are concerned with pastoral teaching, let us
start with a fact of experience which is common to the
vast majority of those who have been engaged in minis-
tering to people. In their reception of the eucharistic
mystery or, as they say, in their communions, benedic-
tions of the Blessed Sacrament, visits to the tabernacle,
and night adorations, few of the faithful have the realization that in and through this mystery, there is truly
a gathering together in God of the Christian community
and of the whole creation. Few of them really understand
that the essence of their spiritual effort in eucharistic

practices must be to enter into a great mystery that exists, in a certain sense, prior to their encounter with it, and that this mystery is the gathering up of all things in Christ and by Christ, in God. This is evident in the communion intentions of the faithful or in the Mass intentions that they offer through their priests. Seldom do these intentions extend beyond the private interests of individuals, even if these are spiritual, for such and such a person living or dead; seldom are they united to the essential catholicity of the eucharistic mystery.

When one draws this to the attention of Christians, their reactions, for all their goodwill, show most often how slight is their knowledge of the objective reality and the scope of the mystery in which they partake. If urged to do better, some will try to improve the interior fervor of their communion. This is then nourished by thoughts of the visit of the friend, of the unworthiness of the dwelling that is offered him, and of the preparations that ought to be made or the thanksgiving immediately after or later on. Others will look rather into what they call precisely their "intentions" at communion and will go to communion *for* this or *for* that, as if they were offering good works and prayers *for* this or *for* that, without reflecting that in this work there is no question of communicating *for* but rather of communicating *with* and communicating *to*, that is, of entering into the great objective mystery which exists prior to their encounter with it, and which is essentially a mystery of universal communion.

Consequently, there are misplaced emphases, if not unmistakable contradictions between the actual spontaneous practice of many believers and the teachings of scripture or the liturgy concerning this mystery. I am speaking not only of the most serious deviations of those who, forgetting the invisible and active presence of Christ in his Church (Mt. 18: 20), which is his body (Eph. 1: 23f.) and to which he continually sends his Spirit (Jn. 14: 17. 26; 16: 13-14; Acts 1: 7-8f.), will unconsciously distort the exact meaning of the eucharistic sacrament, and consider it quite wrongly as the only way or the principal mode of the Lord's presence among us. Nor do I refer to the obvious differences of inspiration that exist between so many "acts before and after communion" and the prayers of the missal, nor the surprise of the faithful and priests in finding the disproportion between the time of thanksgiving and the rest of the Mass, which they look upon as a preparation for communion. There is also that erroneous way of considering the real presence or communion as centered on the communicant or adorer as the final object toward which all the liturgical action tends, and as the ultimate *raison d'être* of the eucharistic mystery.

Let us say now once and for all that there is no question of refusing all justification for this or that particular aspect of the Eucharist. All that we ask is that what is of the essence may not be overlooked. It is quite legitimate and traditional, for example, as shall be amply shown below, to consider communion as one of the privileged moments of personal encounter for the person with his God in and through charity, which is the proper fruit of the sacrament. To celebrate the intimacy of this encounter, one can even borrow the most lyrical expressions of the Canticle of Canticles. But this will depend on respecting the sense of that inspired epithalamium which is to call the presence of God into each communion of love and therefore, not to try to enter into divine intimacy except by previously drawing closer by the same movement of charity in communion with the whole mys-

tery of the People of God. There is no possible intimacy
with God for anyone except by communion with the
Church. In her alone is communicated to men, precisely
by means of the eucharistic mystery, the mystery of the
Holy Spirit which is, in the Church as well as in the
Holy Trinity, the mystery of intimacy and of unity in
love.

Likewise, it is legitimate and fitting that the eucharistic presence be honored with a special worship on
condition that in the worship itself and in its variants,
the essential *raison d'être* of the real presence is respected, namely, the active gathering together of the
whole Church and all creation in the one body of Christ,
which is the Church and ultimately in God. In short,
whatever may be the particular forms of eucharistic worship that is practiced or promoted, one must above all be
careful to preserve in them the essential content of the
mystery that they call forth: the great objective mystery
of the continuous gathering together of the People of
God and of creation under its head, who is Christ.

In the General Movement of the People of God

The People of God: Certainly we have here, on the
concrete level of "economy" where we began, the most
central and synthetic contribution of the Judaeo-Christian
revelation, and one that throws the most light on the
understanding of the majority of the great doctrines of
that revelation. Just as speculative theology should look
at everything by starting with the mystery of the transcendent God, historical theology, which studies revelation
in process, should look at everything from the perspective of the People of God and the continuing development

of this mystery centered on Christ. But to avoid giving a point of view here without justification, we will consider how the teachings of the New Testament show us how to proceed.

I

The Eucharist
as Paschal Mystery

The Eucharist — the Paschal Mystery

Unquestionably, the Lord wanted to put the institution of the Eucharist, which is inseparable from his death and Resurrection within the perspective of the Jewish Pasch.* Although the first explicit teaching concerning this sacrament took place, according to the commonly accepted chronology, about one year before his death (cf. Jn. 6), the institution itself, in spite of his keen desire to introduce it (cf. Lk. 22: 15-16), was accomplished only at the time of the Jewish Pasch on the eve of his own death. He himself explicitly notes the connection: "You know that after two days the Passover is coming, and the Son of man will be delivered up to be crucified" (Mt. 26: 2; cf. also Mk. 14: 1; Lk. 22: 1). He sends his disciples to prepare the Jewish Pasch, which will first be the supper and which *he* intends to transform into "the Pasch of Easter," the new Pasch (cf. Mt. 26:

---

* The French word "Pâque" may also be translated as "Passover" and "Easter"—Trans.

11

17-19; Mk .14: 12, 14, 16; Lk. 22: 7, 8, 11, 13). According to St. Luke, he gave us even then a glimpse of the mysterious immensity and the eschatological duration of this new Pasch: "I have earnestly desired to eat this passover with you before I suffer; for I tell you I shall not eat it until it is fulfilled in the kingdom of God" (Lk. 22: 15-16). St. John also puts the whole catechesis of holy week in the framework of the new Pasch inaugurated by Jesus: "Now before the feast of the Passover, when Jesus knew that his hour had come to depart out of this world to the Father, having loved his own who were in the world, he loved them to the end" (Jn. 13:1). Finally St. Paul follows the same line when he states that "Our Pasch, Christ, has been sacrificed . . ." (1 Cor. 5: 7), and when, by comparing it with the rites of the Jewish Pasch, he attaches to it the duties it entails for Christians following him in this life.

There is, as we have seen, in the words of the Lord, the accounts of the evangelists, and the catechists of St. John or St. Paul, an explicit transfer from the Christian Pasch (the Last Supper and the Passion), to the Jewish Pasch. The substitution of one for the other, we say and pass on quickly to other matters. This is an error in method. It is always worthwhile and on the plane of "economy" as we have defined it, there is even a real necessity to look more closely at these links between the Old and the New Testament. Thus with the help of the figurative teaching of the former, we can truly understand the supernatural realities of the latter.

We should ask ourselves, then, what the Jewish Pasch represents in the history of the People of God. But this means recalling, first of all, the general framework in which this history was written, at least in outline and insofar as it concerns the historical theology of this essay.

Time in the History of the People of God

In the eyes of the believer as well as the historian, the originality of the people of Israel is the way they had, from Abraham to Jesus, of setting themselves up as a people distinct from other peoples through the religious values of which they were the bearers and the guardians. Their ethnic originality—it belongs to the historian to show it—comes neither from their numerical strength, nor their economic resources, nor their military genius, but from their religious beliefs as they are expressed in their laws and as the prophets revived them. Here is their specific genius and profound source of their astonishing vitality. If they are faithful to it, they find in it their principle of cohesion and strength and prosper as a people. If they are unfaithful to it, they soon become aware of the danger of disappearing and being absorbed by neighboring empires. Inversely—and it is the theologian of concrete and historical theology who is more likely to focus on this side of things—it is by means of this people that the religious truths which they possess gradually penetrate mankind, that God, not the God of the philosophers and the learned but the God of Abraham, of Isaac, and of Jacob and finally the God of Jesus Christ, is manifested little by little to men, and that his Word and revelation enter into history and direct its course until that decisive intervention and revelation of God in the historical process which we call the Incarnation.

Now all this historical development of the people of revelation is recorded between two characteristic moments which determine its interpretation. In the beginning launching this people into history by giving them a dynamism are the promises which Abraham heard from

God and which commanded his first migration. At the end, there is the perfect fulfillment of the promises in and by Jesus Christ, toward which the people of God had been progressing since Abraham. Between these two extreme moments their whole history takes place.

Such is the first characteristic of this people. All that takes place between these two moments must be understood in their light, and this light of biblical revelation enlightens the whole history of the People of God from the origins of the world to the end of time. Whether the primary or the secondary object of the promises is considered, the People of God always proceeded, and must always proceed, under pain of ceasing to be itself, in the faith of the promises understood in the past and in the ardent hope of the day when they will begin to be accomplished or terminate or in other words, in fidelity to the contents of a tradition and the basis of an eschatology. This faith and hope, inseparable from each other since they concern the same promises, and inseparable from the historical process since these promises and their accomplishment were and will be inserted in it, are the most fundamental historical and religious endowments of the People of God. The religion of the Jews and the Christians seeks and finds in the history which it later transcends its essential values, namely, the subjective values of faith and hope, events of the past and the future, objective values in a God showing himself in these events and finally, for the Christian faith, God becoming incarnate.

The divine promises which started it all had a double object. First of all, there was the promise of the land of Canaan, a promise fulfilled relatively soon. Next came the promise of the universal blessing for all the families of the earth, numerous as the stars of heaven and the

sands of the sea, a promise of more distant fulfillment
and eschatological import (cf. Gen. 12: 1-3; for the
promise of Canaan: Gen. 12: 7; 13: 14-15; 13: 17;
15: 7; 17: 8; for the universal promise: Gen. 13: 16;
15: 5-6; 17: 1; 18: 17; 22: 16-18). For the historical
duration of the People of God, this gives us the four
principal moments which mark off their history: The
time of Abraham, when the promises were pronounced;
then the time of the Exodus and of the entrance into
Canaan, where the first promise was fulfilled; next, with
the first appearance of the Messiah, the time when the
second, universalist promise began to be realized; lastly,
with the glorious return of the Messiah in his Parousia,
the time of the fulfillment of the second promise and the
fulfillment of the mystery of the People of God. After
this, God, being all in all, "there will be no more time"
(Rev. 10: 6).

These four moments set the limits of the broad sub-
divisions, or periods of historical duration, for the people
of the revelation which scripture usually calls the end of
time. But it is clear that because of the coming of the
Messiah and of the transcendent character of his mystery,
these three periods are of unequal importance, especially
when the first two are compared to the third, or period
of messianic time. The first two from Abraham to Moses
and from Moses to the Messiah should, first of all, be
considered as one, with certain reservations which will
be pointed out later from the point of view of St.
Matthew (1: 18) who distinguishes three stages from
Abraham to David, from David to the Exile, and from the
Exile to Jesus, the Messiah. Concerning the first way of
dividing, scripture speaks of it as one period and as a
time of preparation (Gal. 3: 24) extending from the
promises made to Abraham to the first appearance of the

Messiah, and the other period from the messianic times to the time of fulfillment, or the last days extending from the first appearance of the Messiah to his glorious return. The two—and this is of capital importance for catechesis as well as for historical theology, both of which try to give an account of the "economy"—are distinguished not only by a chronological succession, but by a deeper distinction of a religious condition stemming from the transcendence of the Messiah which brings to the messianic period, or the last days, the realization of a perfect alliance. The period of preparation, however, possesses this alliance only in figure. A still deeper distinction is found. With the Messiah, and because of the transcendent character of his personality and mystery— the mystery of the Incarnation in which the promises made to Abraham are accomplished—the messianic period, or the last days, reach eternity, in a sense, and already contain within themselves, by reason of the same mystery, the transcendent God of the promises. The fact that they continue until the Parousia is merely tangential to this transcendence and eternity.

This is precisely where the mystery of the new and eternal alliance lies, here at the tangent effected by the Incarnation and by grace, whereby the People of God— they entered into eternity by their head which is Chr'st, but still remain in time until the Parousia in their members, the universal descendants promised to Abraham— can by their sacraments and especially by the Eucharist reach their fulfillment by passing continually from time into eternity. But this passing from time into eternity is none other than the mystery of the eucharistic Pasch inaugurated on Calvary and terminating in the Parousia itself. From this first confrontation, we begin to see, in view of the historical economy of the People of God, the vastness of the eucharistic mystery and how it is necessarily coextensive with the whole duration of these last days, or messianic times. "Each time you eat this bread and drink the cup, you proclaim the Lord's death until he comes" (1 Cor. 11: 26).

To arrive at this mystery, one must have passed through the times of preparation which extended from Abraham to Jesus. All those who grant to the messianic era that supernatural relevance characterized by a tangential relation to eternity, all the People of God, all the people of revelation, must do the same. What is the meaning of this period of preparation, and more especially of the three distinct periods? Scripture leaves no doubt about this. In the first place, it teaches us (for example, in the classification of its Hebrew canon, which is more formal in this regard than that of the Septuagint and the Vulgate) that this division is the one that extends from a prophetic period of history starting with the conquest of Canaan to the coming of the Messiah and approaches this coming by the stages of David and the Exile, and the original period when the People of God received its laws, juridical laws to be sure, but also and more basically, laws of a religious establishment which began with those flowing from the promises as mentioned above.

The first of these periods, that of the origins, known principally through the books of the Pentateuch (beginning with Gen. 12: 1), can be called the typological period because it traces the essential characteristics which, with due proportion guarded in transfering them to messianic times, will be those of the People of God until the end of time. The second period, which begins with Joshua, and the third, which starts with the infidelities of Jeroboam and Ahab, and is followed by the punishment of exile, can be called prophetic periods because all the factors at work converge toward the future and at the end toward the messianic mysteries. Joshua is great because he belongs both to the first and second periods (for this reason sometimes the word "Hexateuch" is substituted for Pentateuch), and that is why rather than because of his name he is the first great prototype of the Messiah: As the latter but on a different plane, it is in fulfilling the promises of God that he gives to Israel along with the land of Canaan their status as the People of God. They are truly the People of God only when God begins to give them the realization of his promises.

Typology of the Time of Preparation

Whether it be a question of the first, or typological period, or whether it be a question of the two others, the prophetic periods, scripture tells us that the sacred history within them was valuable not only as preparation but also as a prefiguration of the last days, or messianic times, and the supernatural mysteries which were to be accomplished during them. "Now these things happened to them as a warning, but they were written down for our instruction, upon whom the end of the ages has come" (1 Cor. 10: 11). From then on, the Old Testament events and their providential unfolding seem like an immense and realistic divine discourse, not in words but in deeds, in which we can discover the meaning of the mysteries of the New Testament.

If it is in the New Covenant that the Lord realizes his intentions, it is in the Old that he begins not only to prepare his people but to manifest them fully. Consequently, one can only approach an understanding of New Testament mysteries properly by lending an attentive ear to the teachings of the Old, unless one is to reject more or less explicitly the teaching that God himself wanted to give his people. So it is in our case. When the Lord was about to institute the Eucharist, and wanted to tell us how to approach the mystery, he presented it in the context of the Jewish Pasch and wanted us to understand the Eucharist in terms of it. Likewise, by choosing bread and wine for the institution of his Eucharist, he closely related it to the sacrifice of Melchizedek. The whole history of the people of revelation is intended to clarify the meaning of the eucharistic mystery.

The eucharistic Pasch, we begin to see, merely *realizes* according to the supernatural *relevance* proper to messianic times, or the last days, what the Jewish Pasch first prefigured in the days of preparation.

The Typological Meaning of the Exodus Cycle

The Jewish Pasch first makes its appearance as one of the elements of the Exodus cycle and must consequently be understood as a function of it. The guiding lines are noteworthy in this cycle, which is certainly one of the most typological of this period of the old revelation.

Besides the narratives which the piety of Israel has preserved in the biblical accounts, the cycle of the Exodus seems to include the three characteristic moments that are mentioned below, which, in turn, have a teaching value for all subsequent history and for the mystery of the People of God. In the first instance, we see the departure from Egypt, the land of slavery and at the conclusion the taking possession of Canaan, the promised land. Between the two events, we find the crossing of the desert which separated one land from the other.

The land of Egypt during the time of Joseph had been for Israel a land of economic riches and demographic increase (cf. Gen. 45: 17-20; 46: 3; 47: 11; 50: 20; Exod. 1: 13-14; 2: 23; 3: 7-8). From this enslavement and this idolatry, God alone could rescue the Hebrews (cf. Exod. 13: 36; 13: 96; 13: 166; 20: 2; Deut. 7: 8, 18-19; Ps. 106: 8). He did this by the extraordinary and well-known intervention which impressed the wise men of Egypt and showed what a difference there is for Yahweh between Egypt and Israel (Exod. 11: 7). At all times, the People of God will have to be rescued by him from serving the idols of this world.

For the people en route to the promised land the desert was the period of improvement and decline. It was a time of improvement at Sinai because of the step forward in God's revelation of his mystery to his people (cf. Exod. 3: 13f.; 6: 3), the establishment of the Covenant (cf. Exod. 19: 5-6), the promulgation of the Decalogue and the holy Law and through all this, the time of singular nearness of God and his people, whom he was leading and nourishing. The decline consisted of the long series of infidelities of the people from the adoration of the golden calf to the prostitution of the daughters of Moab (Num. 25: 1-16) to the great apostasies of Kadesh and the sin of Moses himself against Yahweh (Num. 20: 2f.). Because of the infidelities of the people and those favors of God, the desert is, above all, the time of purification and last minute preparations necessary for entering into the Canaanite heritage of the promises. This stage will also be necessary for the people of God in its progress towards the eschatological object of these same promises.

Finally, the conquest of the promised land by Joshua is the mystery, at first sight paradoxical, of a free gift of

God which has to be taken by force by those who receive it and who rely on the strength of the God living within them. Here we find the whole theme of the Book of Joshua: God stirring up within his people their strong energies so that they can freely take possession of the free gift that God begins to make to them according to his promises.

Because they belong to an intensely typological period of the history of People of God, these three essential times of the movement of the Exodus have made durable marks which will remain characteristic of the people until the end of time. The original circumstances of this period, in which the true birth of his people was accomplished, have, as it were, fixed for them the true laws of nature. That is why tradition still keeps these accounts in the books of the Laws. The People of God will always have to be liberated by God's omnipotence from the world of slavery and idolatry, while they carry toward the promised land all the riches which they may have found in the world they are leaving. They will always have to pass through the purifications of the desert which, by the gratuitous mercy of God who tried to become their ally and in spite of their unceasing infidelities, will be the great benefit derived from their nomad wanderings in this world. Strong with the power of the living God within them, they will always have to use all their resources of energy and liberty to conquer like Joshua, the true and definitive promised land. There is no need to insist that these themes are classical in patristic literature and in the liturgy.

But all this which in the figurative history of the time of preparation is inaugurated with the Pasch that opens the cycle of the Exodus is consummated in the supernatural order of messianic times by the Pasch of the new and eternal Covenant, that is, by the eucharistic Pasch, of which the first was only the figure. To enter fully into an understanding of the eucharistic Pasch, we must see this new stage in closer relation to what was in the figurative cycle of the Exodus, the Pasch of Moses, by which the cycle was opened.

The Pasch of the Exodus

The Pasch of Egypt is composed, first, of the immolation of a lamb (cf. Exod. 12: 3f.), the blood of which would preserve Israel from the chastisement merited by the stiff-necked idolatrous Egyptians and which would descend on them at the vengeful passing of Yahweh (cf. Exod. 12: 7; 12: 12f.; 12: 22-23). Then follows an essentially communal and sacred meal in which the whole People of God, in haste to depart, stand with shoes on their feet and staffs in their hands, and consume the flesh of a lamb (cf. Exod. 12: 11). At this meal, moreover, there will be bread which in their haste the people have not had time to leaven and bitter herbs contrasting with the delicious onions of Egypt, for which they so often longed in the desert. From the unfermented dough which they began to eat on that Pasch of the departure, they also cooked unleavened cakes during the first days of their wandering march (cf. Exod. 12: 39), and afterwards had the miraculous manna (cf. Exod. 16: 13f). And this will not stop falling until after the celebration of the first Pasch in the promised land (cf. Josh. 5: 12).

Here again, from amid details some dominant facts emerge. First of all, there are those that concern the People of God. There is no need to insist on these because they are so obvious. The Pasch is a mystery in which the

People of God must participate as a whole, and none except the members of this people can participate in it. The Book of Exodus insists strongly on this (cf. Exod. 12: 43-49). Only the Israelites can eat the paschal meal and benefit from the protection of the blood of the lamb. No Egyptian or foreigner can claim it unless he had been previously accepted into the people of the circumcision (cf. Exod. 12: 44).

On his side, the Israelite himself can not claim it except in union with the totality of his people. The Pasch is not an individual rite: It is celebrated by the whole people in one and the same movement of liberation and in one and the same passing from the slavery and idolatry of Egypt to the liberty of the desert and the Covenant with Yahweh.

This "one and the same movement" is the principal characteristic. Everything in these paschal rites is evocative of movement, of the passage of God amid men, who bring to pass in their own history the punishment of the stiff-necked, idolatrous Egyptians and the marvelous liberation of themselves, the People of God, whom this very passage sends forth towards the fulfillment of the promises. The immolation of the lamb marks the first passage and initiates the first movement. This passage and movement of the people of Israel out of the land of slavery and to the promised land which is inaugurated by the paschal meal will continue until the day of the division of the land of Canaan among the tribes.

Yet, we cannot remain content with considering only the external appearances of this migration of the Hebrews. It is easy to imagine the powerful desire, at once patriotic and religious, animating this migration which carried them towards the land of the patriarchs and the joy in which they celebrated this Pasch of their liberation. This joy will mark the celebration of the Pasch throughout the history of this people until it is superseded by the more joyous, eucharistic Pasch that liberates from servitude more definitively and is closer to their inheritance.

But that is not all. Not only is it essential to the Pasch itself to be a movement, and a passage, but it also seems that for this very reason it is at the heart of the very movement of the People of God and necessarily marks in a way the stages of their history. It is what made them pass simultaneously from Egypt to Canaan and, from the typological to the prophetical period. From that day onward, the Pasch would serve as a point of departure in their chronology, as well as the commemoration, marking the beginning of each year (cf. Exod. 12: 1; 12: 6). Finally, it will be celebrated at each renewal of the Covenant or the Law with a greater solemnity, as if to say that this new departure could not take place except in view of, and with, the impetus of the liberation and the conquest which had permanently been accomplished by the Pasch of Egypt. Except for the first Pasch of Joshua, which was really only a conclusion of that of Exodus (cf. Josh. 5: 10), we can find examples of this in the solemn Paschs of the time Hezekiah (cf. 2 Chr. 30: 15f.), and of Josiah (cf. 2 Chr. 35: 1f.).

Moreover, it is not a question here of chronology or of external solemnities only. The mystery of the Pasch directs the movement of the People of God in time and in history, first of all, because it creates or maintains in souls a profound spiritual and religious movement. With the sabbath and the circumcision, and perhaps more so, the Pasch was the great religious institution of Israel, which sustained in its people the richest inspirations and the most characteristic beliefs.

This is true, first of all, in their liturgy. The Pasch of Egypt, and more especially the immolation of the lamb, is commemorated by the obligatory consecration to Yahweh of the firstborn, of men as well as of animals (cf. Exod. 13: 1-2; 13: 11-16; Num. 3: 13; 8: 17). Still richer in suggestion of the past and of greater spiritual intensity was the Pasch celebrated each year as the most sacred of feasts. This one marked the beginning of the new year and the renewal of souls, lasted a whole week during which nothing else was done, and required a radical purification of men and things. It also recalled to the People of God their perpetual condition in history of being on a journey, and pointed to the future and the fulfillment of the ultimate promises as well as to the past and their entrance into the inheritance of the first promises. As time progressed, the messianic hope became uppermost in the celebration of the Pasch and took precedence over the mere recollection of the past. Evidently, even in the darkest moments of the exile, for example, the most pious Jews had the foresight to expect a great and lasting messianic Pasch, as hoped for by the prophets (cf. for example: Is. 12: 1-6; 52: 8-10; Jer. 31:10-14; 50: 3, 14-20; Ps. 96; 98).

The Eucharistic Pasch

In this paschal tradition, still very much alive in the religion of his people according to the Gospel accounts, Jesus will introduce the new Pasch. We have already pointed out a few of the characteristics by which he obviously intended to emphasize this continuity. These appear in his teaching. But it is most clearly seen in the fact that in spite of his ardent desire to institute the new

Pasch (cf. Lk. 22: 15), he waits for the Jewish Pasch to do so. There is continuity therefore instead of substitution, outgrowth instead of abolition. Prefigurations and preparations are replaced by realities: "... it was not Moses who gave you the bread from heaven; my Father gives you the true bread from heaven" (Jn. 6: 32). The new and eternal covenant replaces the first and gives it a final meaning, that is, its fulfillment, just as previously the sermon on the Mount, far from dissolving the Law and the prophets, had achieved their fulfillment (cf. Mt. 5: 17).

To one who approaches it thus in its continuity with the Jewish Pasch, the Pasch of Jesus presents two quite general characteristics that must be considered before analyzing the elements that compose it.

The first characteristic will be described in the Christian Church as a eucharistic Pasch. The texts of the New Testament, and those especially which concern the Last Supper, emphasize the importance of thanksgiving in the soul of Our Lord as he instituted the sacrament. One would say that it was the dominating note in this instance. In the celebration of the Jewish Pasch there had certainly been formulas of blessings, and Our Lord pronounced them at the Last Supper (*eulogesas:* cf. Mt. 26: 26; Mk. 14: 22). There were also hymns at the conclusion which were none other than Psalms 113 to 118, and the Lord intoned them (*hymnesantes:* cf. Mt. 26: 30; Mk. 14: 26). But there is no doubt that Jesus added the enthusiastic expression of an act of thanksgiving bearing more directly on the prolongation of the traditional Pasch, and already expressing one of the essential aspects of it, the one which its name will express in the future. This also appears in the accounts of the synoptics (cf. Mt. 26: 27; Mk. 14: 23; Lk. 22: 17) and in St. Paul (cf. 1 Cor. 11: 24). Furthermore, if the very term (*eucharistesas*) is also employed in the account of the multiplication of the loaves (cf. Mt. 15: 36; Mk. 8: 6; Jn. 6: 11; 6: 23), one should not forget that it has a close relation to the Eucharist according to St. John, and that this is expressed in all the early Christian iconography.

Why this act of thanksgiving and what is its importance? Precisely because at the Last Supper the Pasch ceased to be a figure and became an accomplished fact. With the Last Supper and cross — inseparable as we shall see later — the People of God left the era of preparation and entered into their promised inheritance. The new and eternal covenant succeeded the Mosaic Covenant. At that moment, all that the People of God had desired and called for since the Pasch of the Exodus and even since the promises made to Abraham, all their past dissatisfaction (the history of their faults and the reproofs of their prophets) and the longing it had implanted, all the messianism, in a word, which more and more explicitly had directed the best of their just men towards the future, all this began to be fulfilled on that day. From then on why should not the Messiah, who before partaking, first recalled reverently all the religious past and the aspirations of his people, speak words of thanksgiving when their aspirations were on the point of being fulfilled, and when the past was at last coming to an end? In that very hour—his hour, the one for which he had come (cf. Jn. 7: 30; 8: 20; 13: 1)—when he was to pass out of this world (cf. Jn. 13: 1) and when by virtue of this very passing, the real and efficacious Pasch of the New Covenant was replacing the figurative Pasch of the Exodus, the Messiah could only offer thanks in accord with the deepest desires of his people and

especially his own (cf. Lk. 22: 15). He offered thanksgiving, then, for the realization of what was awaited, for
the accomplishment of what was promised, for the consummation of what had only been hinted at and prefigured. The last days or the time of plenitude being hereby
inaugurated, each Pasch would henceforth preserve as
its most basic characteristic the exultation and gratitude
which the fulfillment of divine promises calls forth from
men. Every Pasch would be primarily eucharistic.

On the other hand, since the last days were only in-
cipiently a time of plenitude, every Pasch would still
retain something of the desire and movement of the
Pasch of the preparation period, with this important difference, that the movement and the desire would no
longer focus on the inauguration of the messianic Covenant, already inaugurated with Calvary and the Resurrection, but on the consummation of this Covenant.
Every Pasch of the latter days would necessarily be
eucharistic and eschatological (cf. 1 Cor. 11: 26).
Before him, our Lord himself had explicitly mentioned
this. "I have desired to eat this passover with you before
I suffer" (Lk. 22: 15), he had said to his disciples. And
immediately he added the following, which in this
paschal perspective took on an eschatological meaning:
"For I tell you that from now on I shall not drink of the
fruit of the vine until the kingdom of God comes" (Lk.
22: 16), and in St. Matthew: "I tell you I shall not drink
again of this fruit of the vine until that day when I
drink it new with you in my Father's kingdom" (Mt.
26: 29).

We begin to see at this point the whole eschatological
duration of the latter days as the time for the unfolding
of this new Pasch. And this amounts to saying that the
Eucharist, the consummation and fulfillment of the fig-

urative Pasch of the Exodus—for this reason it cannot help being eucharistic and yet it does not put an end to the development of the Paschal mystery—is necessarily eschatological. According to what we have said about the supernatural relevance proper to the latter days, the development of the Paschal mystery continues henceforth not only on the historical plane but also on that of participation of supernatural realities, which are the true objects of the ultimate promises. Here, we see that the Pasch inaugurated in the Cenacle will not be completed until the Parousia, when the whole People of God will thereby have, in the inheritance of the promises, completed this passing which their Messiah first inaugurated for them. In other words, as the Pasch of the Exodus was not really completed until the passover of Joshua into the promised land (cf. Jos. 5: 12), so the eucharistic Pasch of Jesus will not be consummated until the kingdom of his Father is not only inaugurated (this has been true since the first coming of the Messiah and in every Eucharist) but completed and glorious as it will be at the time of the Parousia. Every Eucharist reaches impatiently toward that time when he will return. Only then will there be inaugurated by the glorious Messiah surrounded by his people a new (cf. Mt. 26: 29) and eternal Pasch which is, no doubt that passage of the Son to the Father eternally is prolonged in the Holy Trinity by Him of whom St. John speaks when he begins the account of the Last Supper (cf. Jn. 13: 1).

We can now discuss in its essential elements and not only in the perspective of the figurative Pasch, that eucharistic Pasch of which we know the general characteristics and of which we are beginning to grasp the supernatural relevance.

II

The Eucharist
as Paschal Meal

Paschal Meal and Paschal Immolation

In the Pasch of the Exodus and in its yearly commemoration, the immolation of the lamb preceded the paschal meal and furnished the principal food for it. This is the way it was certainly in the first part of the Last Supper of the Lord, the purely Jewish part which the apostles were told to prepare and which was carried out by Jesus and his followers according to traditional rites (cf. Mt. 26: 17-19; Mk. 14: 12-16; Lk. 22: 7-13). In fact, we see at the Last Supper the presence of the dish of sacrificed meat (cf. Jn. 13: 26). It was in the course of this meal "as they were eating" (cf. Mt. 26: 26 and parallel passages) that Jesus, changing the normal ritual of tradition in order to establish his own, took bread and wine and instituted in the act of thanksgiving the new Pasch considered in its original element, that is, as a eucharistic meal. Of this new Pasch, the second element was to be the Passion (and what it entailed inseparably: the Resurrection, Ascension, and sending

31

of the Holy Spirit), just as it was announced at that very moment by the words of consecration.

By the same token, the notable difference between the Jewish Pasch and the Christian Pasch is manifested. In the first one, it is after the immolation of the victim that the people approach the meal by which they begin to enter into the act of their liberation. In the second, on the contrary, they had to begin by participation in the eucharistic meal in order to approach after that the mystery of the sacrifice to which the meal leads directly. The Lord himself seems to have respected this sequence in his approach to the mystery of his sacrifice. He could have instituted the Eucharist at one of the meals which followed his resurrection, but did not, and it is clear that the order chosen by him—supper first and Passion following—corresponded in his case, as it should in ours, with the profound exigencies of the new Pasch. Whether this was done with a pedagogical intention to teach us how to enter into the mystery of his Passion or whether and more profoundly, it was because of internal exigencies that he himself had to obey, it seems clear that while passing by way of the Paschal meal, we are invited to join in the mystery of the immolation. This is the normal order of the new passage, of this new Pasch.

The Azyme in Exodus

The material used is all the more impressive because if we consider the new paschal meal in itself, we find there a new element differing from the old. Whereas in the Jewish paschal meal the immolated lamb was the principal ingredient (the azyme and the bitter herbs were only side dishes with a predominantly symbolic value), in the Christian Pasch it is the bread and wine which first appear as central.

What is this bread and wine, and what is the meaning of this partially new rite which the Lord instituted in this way during the last Jewish Pasch? Evidently, what is immediately obvious is that the bread of the Christian Pasch is the prolongation of that of the Jewish Pasch. The azyme in the latter becomes the eucharistic bread in the former, and the original symbolism of the first (the unleavened bread in the haste of departure, of the passage) is continued for the benefit of the second. The eucharistic bread is still essentially a paschal bread, a bread of passage, that is, of a departure, a liberation, a march toward a beyond. Like the manna which continued the benefits, it is a bread that sustains the People of God in their crossing of the desert towards the promised land. "... it was not Moses who gave you the bread from heaven," Jesus had said. "My Father gives you the true bread from heaven" (Jn. 6: 31-32). "Your fathers ate the manna in the wilderness, and they died" (Jn. 6: 49). "He who eats this bread will live for ever" (Jn. 6: 58).

The Bread and Wine of Melchizedek

But the Christian Eucharist seems to go beyond this and its first and immediate biblical root in the Mosaic Pasch too often causes us to overlook another which seems no less certain and which is surely of greater importance. The provision for the Christian Pasch is not bread alone, but bread and wine together. But what could this call to the minds of Jews nourished in the biblical culture, as were the disciples of Jesus? What would they think of this rite that their master abruptly introduced in the midst of the traditional Pasch as the essential rite of the new Pasch? In the days before the Mosaic rites, henceforth superseded as the Epistle to the Hebrews says, had there not been another more ancient rite, performed by a priest who was not a descendant of Aaron, a rite all the more worthy of respect and laden with mystery in that it belonged to the cycle of Abraham, a rite which also made use of bread and wine, the rite of Melchizedek? (Gen. 14: 18-20).

The similarity was all the more impressive because in Psalm 110, the messianic Psalm that Jesus himself had spoken of quite recently and decisively (cf. Mt. 22: 41-46), the Messiah was represented as exercising the priesthood of Melchizedek, whose only known rite was precisely the offering of bread and wine which he made one day to the People of God in the person of the patriarch, Abraham.

But the similarity does not end here. In the episode recounted in Genesis and in the Gospel accounts of the Last Supper, the offering of bread and wine is made within the context of the blessing and thanksgiving for the decisive victory of the people who had received the promises over their enemies (cf. Gen. 14: 20). In the Genesis account, the offering is made to Abraham or to his later descendents, the people of the promises by the priest, Melchizedek, whose origins are mysterious. In the Gospel accounts, it is made by the priest, Jesus, whose origins are even more mysterious (thus his title as priest according to the order of Melchizedek). (Cf. Mt. 22: 41-46.) For one who tries to realize, by means of the texts and going beyond the texts, what the Last Supper was in its concrete unfolding and in its power of biblical evocation, the passages in the Epistle to the Hebrews on the priesthood of Jesus, a priesthood not at all according to Aaron but "according to the order of Melchizedek," do not seem groundless, but solidly founded on evangelical facts, notably on this offering of bread and wine. They set the pattern in a fully authentic way for the eucharistic theology required by these themes (cf. Heb. 5: 6; 5: 10; 6: 20; 7: 1; 7: 10; 7: 15; 7: 17).

Let us go even further along the path opened by these considerations. The immolated meat belongs to the Mosaic cycle and the stage that it represents in the development of the People of God. This development, following a law which is valid for all human collectivities, took place in the direction of complexity and elaboration of the rites. In contrast, what we know of what is called the sacrifice of Melchizedek appears to be connected with a human and religious way of living that is still very simple and close to the elementary realities of nature; one might almost say it is spiritual.

The offering of bread and the wine that Melchizedek presented to Abraham in a religious and hospitable gesture was, in fact, more spiritual and close to natural simplicity than all the sacred butcherings which the Mosaic laws prescribed. Comparing the Christian sacrifice to the sacrifices of the Temple, the Fathers of the Church (and before that the Epistle to the Hebrews 13: 9ff.) tended to point out the crudeness of the latter and the spiritual quality of the former. The remark is equally valid when comparing them to the rite of Melchizedek. To tell the truth, it seems that it was the rite of the time of the patriarchs that Christ, the priest according to the order of Melchizedek, uniting himself once again with the cycle of Abraham and passing over that of Moses, wanted to borrow as a paschal rite for messianic times.

But what was the meaning of this distant rite? And

does this meaning carry over in its adaptation in the Christian Eucharist? In offering bread and wine to Abraham, Melchizedek pronounced this formula of benediction: "Blessed be Abram by God Most High, maker of heaven and earth" (Gen. 14: 19). It has often been pointed out that this formula of Melchizedek bespeaks a religion that is not at all particularist as those of the clans about him, but one that is cosmic and universalist. The God of Melchizedek is God the creator of heaven and earth, and it is in the name of this God that the king-priest offers these humble and elementary products of the earth—bread and wine. To partake of these offerings is for him and for Abraham his guest, a communion, not only with each other but also and in a certain way with the creator of heaven and earth in whose worship, even though they are chiefs of two clans ethnically different, they have met that day. Naming the God of Melchizedek will henceforth be to name the God of Abraham.

Priest According to the Order of Melchizedek

These profound and somewhat primitive values are certainly found again in the matter chosen by Jesus, the priest according to the order of Melchizedek, for the eucharistic meal of the new Pasch. After one has understood that in preference to the complications of the ritual so highly evolved and involved as the Mosaic ritual was, he chose to recapture the simplicity of patriarchal times and the purity of their great religious inspirations, especially after one has perceived how much he loved that creation in which his Father chose to place men, one has no doubt that he preferred to the bloody and roasted sacrifices of the Jews the good bread and the beautiful wine of vineyards as matter for that sacrament which through them and through itself makes all things pass into communion with the creator of heaven and earth. "The earth is the Lord's, and everything in it," St. Paul reminds us in a text where he is actually inviting the faithful of Corinth to thank God for all food (cf. 1 Cor. 10: 25-30).

Better than sacrificed meats, the bread and wine "formerly scattered over the hills and now become one" (Did. 9: 9) appear as food, and by eating it, men give homage to the creator of heaven and earth for all this material universe which slowly prepared it for them. It is not unknown that from St. Irenaeus and St. Cyril up to Teilhard de Chardin this cosmic dimension of the eucharistic mystery has captivated many religious people. The Byzantine liturgies also bring this out forcefully when they remind us at the consecration of the accounts of the creation of the world in the first chapters of Genesis.

The cosmic as well as the human dimension is here. Just as material creation required centuries of evolution and slow germination to prepare the wheat and the fruit of the wine, so men were needed to transform by their labor wheat and grapes into the bread and wine they consumed in their meals together. Because labor has established some bonds of union between men and because bread is the fruit of their labor, to offer bread to someone as Melchizedek did to Abraham is to offer him a share in this work and to establish bonds with him. One lives for his work and the fruit he derives from it. Thus, whenever we nourish a person with this fruit, we communicate our lives to him.

Hence the seriousness, and religious significance of

every act of hospitality and every meal eaten together. Hence also the particularly odious character of any betrayal by a former guest, of any meanness from one who shared your bread. "He who ate my bread has lifted his heel against me" (Jn. 13: 18; Ps. 41: 10). And again: "But behold the hand of him who betrays me is with me on the table" (Lk. 22: 21). The hateful betrayal of Judas was intensified by the fact that he did it after a meal which was essentially a meal of communion: the first paschal meal of universal communion of the People of God in messianic times.

Even now we glimpse the presence of these human and deeply religious values in this communion by bread and wine to which Melchizedek invited Abraham, as well as in the one according to the same rite and inspiration to which Jesus invited his disciples. As we proceed, even higher values of communion will be revealed to us in the Christian Pasch. Let them not cause us to fail to realize the beauty of the earlier rite however primitive and elementary it may seem to us. Considering all this in the context of human labor today and of contemporary economic systems, we could never begin to realize in the complexity of their interaction the number of relationships and interchanges synthesized in the hosts that become the bread of our eucharistic meals.

By considering the matter chosen by the Lord for the new Pasch, we are led unawares to perspectives of human and even universal communion which we shall see more deeply when we investigate the spiritual import of this paschal meal.

One final remark, however, can be made here. Once we see that the movement, or passage, in God begins to take on recognizable shape in the depths of humanity and the universe, where the material for the paschal meal is formed, it becomes evident that in this rudimentary area of preparation, the law, so to speak, of gathering all things together bears out in favor of the People of God in this Pasch, which sets in motion the movement toward the accomplishment of the promises. It is truly, even in this ordering of the elements of the cosmic universe, a moment linked to the power of the enemy of God: If we consider only the matter of the Christian Pasch, everything appears to us as leading onward, in passage, not only with regard to duration, but in its very being and finality, to a mystery of accomplishment which is nothing other than what St. Paul calls the mystery of the recapitulation of all things, including the universe, in Christ (cf. Eph. 1: 10).

The Paschal Meal of Fraternal Communion

In the time of preparation, as we said, the Jewish Pasch was that of the whole people, but only of the chosen people. Neither the Egyptian nor the foreigner took part in it. The particularism of their election also involved their Pasch and communion. In the messianic period on the contrary, the time for the fulfillment of the universalist promises made to Abraham, the people of the Messiah no longer recognized particularism. The Pasch was now offered with every right to all men of goodwill (cf. Lk. 2: 14). The wedding banquet, disdained by those who had first been invited, was opened to the throng of poor, weak, blind, and lame (cf. Lk. 14: 22), the good and the bad (cf. Mt. 22: 10). By the same token, all men are also invited to partake of the new paschal meal: "Drink of it, all of you," Jesus insists as he hands around the cup (Mt. 26: 27).

That the Last Supper was essentially a communion meal is too obvious to require lengthy demonstration. This was already the meaning of the Jewish Pasch, as was said. But even more is it the meaning of the Christian Pasch. Many things bring this out. For example, the Lord reveals the ardor of his own charity by telling his disciples about the desire that he had to eat the Pasch with them (cf. Lk. 22: 15); his love goes to the extreme of making him their servant and washing their feet (cf. Jn. 13: 1f.); he exhorts them in his great farewell discourse to love one another in the same way as he (Jn. 13: 12f.). He also addresses the sacerdotal prayer to his Father which is focused on unity and which makes almost palpably present at that moment, not only the immediate disciples, but those who until the end of time "will believe in me through their word" (cf. Jn. 17: 1-20). Everything in the Last Supper is a mystery of communion of bodies in the same bread and in the same wine which are the body and blood of the Messiah. Also and more profoundly, it is a mystery of communion of souls in the unity and totality of the members of the messianic people.

The Tragedy of Judas

The tragedy of Judas and the gravity of his fault stems precisely from his betrayal, in which he separates himself not only from the Messiah but also from the whole messianic people at the time when the communion of the universal people is about to be consummated in the one who introduced it by the new Pasch into the inheritance of the definitive promises. The Gospel points up this climax and the exact nature of this tragic spiritual drama when it shows Judas accepting without repenting or acknowledging his incipient treason the morsel Jesus offered him as a sign of communion. "Then after the morsel, Satan entered into him" (Jn. 13: 27). His tragedy is to have willed the betrayal of the Messiah exactly when he was invited to enter as all the others into the universal communion of the messianic people that the new Pasch was about to realize. "He who is not with me is against me, and he who does not gather with me scatters. Therefore I tell you, every sin and blasphemy will be forgiven men, but the blasphemy against the Spirit will not be forgiven. And whoever says a word against the Son of man will be forgiven; but whoever speaks against the Holy Spirit will not be forgiven, either in this age or the age to come" (Mt. 12: 30-32).

Although Judas on the eve of the Last Supper had spoken against the Son of Man, he could still be forgiven. But he brought his treason even to the heart of the paschal meal of the messianic people. This treason was opposed, precisely because it was in it, to the universal communion which the meal was going to accomplish. His betrayal was affirmed in his soul precisely in the gesture of communion. He received the morsel that Jesus offered him and shortly afterwards, by a mark of love, a kiss, betrayed his Master. All this in his soul amounts to blasphemy against the Holy Spirit and against charity, the very soul of the messianic people. The liturgy of Holy Thursday points out this striking contrast and shows the point by point opposition of the mystery of the Last Supper and the mystery of Judas. It is precisely from the point of view of communion that they are inseparable one from the other and explain each other.

But is it true that Judas was present at the time of the institution of the new Pasch? This seems as unlikely considering the mysteries involved and improbable from the point of view of exegesis. It was at the close of the Jewish part of the supper that he consummated by the morsel he treacherously accepted from his Master the blasphemous betrayal of the Messiah and of the communion of the messianic people. This betrayal could go as far as the threshold of the messianic times and mysteries, but could not enter there. In itself, this first Christian Pasch, of which all the other sacred meals until the Parousia would only extend the efficacity for a universal gathering, could only be flawless. Judas could not compromise this efficacity from within. Had he chosen to remain at the Last Supper, he could have experienced its benefits himself and could have entered into its liberating action. "So, after receiving the morsel, he immediately went out; and it was night" (Jn. 13: 30). Of his own accord by betraying fraternal charity, Judas had withdrawn himself from the liberating action of the new Pasch.

The Eucharistic Consecration
and the Charity of the Body of Christ

After this, charity of the gathering was without flaw, and the Lord could proceed to institute the new Pasch. It is all important to this institution to find the atmosphere of charity and fraternal affection in which Jesus wanted to approach it. Above, we recalled the principal facts by which he first created this atmosphere. For the new Pasch, even more than for that of the Exodus, there had to be, first of all, a fraternal meal in which all the members of the People of God (on the point of the passing over into the promised inheritance, formerly organized by Moses, now by Jesus) become aware of their interdependence, and strengthen their solidarity. Over the one cup passing from hand to hand among the disciples as a sign of their communion and over the one bread divided among them for all to eat, the words of consecration fell. They did not create the bread and the wine that they consecrated nor did they create the fraternal communion of the disciples; rather, they assumed them along with the bread and wine into a higher mystery. Out of this solidarity of his disciples in fraternal love the words really made his body, which is the Church, just as he made his body and blood out of the bread and wine. And just as bread and wine had to be prepared for the institution of the new Pasch, the disciples who were to enter into it had to prepare by strengthening the bonds of charity.

In the paschal meal of the New Covenant these two aspects must never be dissociated, that of the mystical body, as it will later be referred to, and that of his eucharistic body. It is by the genuine fraternal charity in the former that one approaches the reality of the latter. Just as in the new Law one must first be reconciled with one's brother before presenting one's offering at the altar (cf. Mt. 5: 23-24), so in the new Pasch one must pass from the fraternal meal of the Cenacle to reach by the consecration of bread and wine the mysteries of Calvary. This is the normal progression of the mystery of the Pasch.

Thus, the scandal of St. Paul when he learns that the faithful in Corinth are not observing fraternal charity with one another, and, what is more, they are failing to do so at the very time of the Lord's Supper: "For in eating, each one goes ahead with his own meal, and one is hungry and another is drunk" (1 Cor. 11: 21). If you only come to eat, he continues in substance, you would

do better to stay in your homes! That is no longer the
meal the Lord wanted, which is essentially a fraternal
meal. Or else, he continues, if you transform it into a
meal that is wholly material where one eats and where
one drinks, it is perhaps because you are deliberately
despising the assembly of God, the Church of God, and
especially those with it who should have a preferential
charity, the poor and the needy (cf. 1 Cor. 11: 22). In
that case, when after your selfish meal you partake of
the eucharistic bread and drink the blood of the chalice,
tell yourself that it is in an unworthy fashion (cf. 1 Cor.
11: 27f.) and this will not escape the severe judgment of
God (cf. 1 Cor. 11: 29). This development shows clearly
once again that it is by passing from the fraternal meal
of the Christian community that one approaches the
eucharistic mysteries of the body and blood of the Lord.
The Christian Pasch, as the Pasch of the Exodus is only
consumed in the fraternal and liberating meal of the
whole people of God.

In fact, there is no doubt that in the early days of the
Christians, the eucharistic celebration was, first of all,
this: a meal in common in which Christians drew closer
together in fraternal charity in Christ made present in
their midst by that charity itself (cf. Mt. 18: 20) before
the presence wrought by the eucharistic consecration
drew them more deeply into the paschal mystery.
Whether these fraternal meals referred back to the Last
Supper as in the Paulinian eucharists, or whether they
were instead a reenactment of those meals that the risen
Jesus had taken with his disciples, as seems to be the
case in the breaking of the bread in the Acts of the
Apostles, they could differ according to the aspect of this
paschal mystery which they more particularly evoked,
but at least they all had this in common: They were

fraternal meals which, first of all, strengthened the communion in which they knew themselves to be and their unity with the whole Church.

The first effect of the eucharistic bread itself was to signify—before consecrating it and thereby strengthening it—this unity of all in charity. "Because there is one bread, we who are many are one body, for we all partake of the one bread" (1 Cor. 10: 17). For a long while, we know, some eucharistic rites which have now disappeared and which tried to emphasize more the fraternal communion essential to the Eucharist rather than to surround it with respect expressed in a very impressive way the feeling they had of unity with the whole Church in the Lord's supper. The ceremony of the *fractio* and the *fermentum* manifested its unity by spreading it over space; the ceremony of the *sancta* manifested its unity over the passage of time. No Christian, of course, would have dreamed of separating himself from his brethren, that is, from the Church to partake of the eucharistic Pasch.

The Joy of the Christian Meal

From this stems the joy of those agapes, not an exuberant joy, but a profound joy of the heart and soul which is only tasted in friendship. "And day by day, attending the temple together and breaking bread in their homes, they partook of food with glad and generous hearts" (Acts 2: 46). Joy—theology will explain later— is the proper fruit of charity; we mean by this, fraternal charity in the exchanges of which Christians found God himself present. It is an essentially eucharistic joy, more- over, in the sense in which we have defined this word above, that is, the joy of the People of God realizing that they have entered into the last days or the messianic time of fulfilled promises, the joy which continues that of the Messiah among his own at the Last Supper and which, as that one, leads to the Eucharist of the paschal mystery.

This fraternal and eucharistic joy of the Christian suppers, of which the action was continued and transcended in accomplishing the eucharistic mystery, appears to have been so habitual in the first days of Christianity that it seems to have been found even in ordinary meals that were not crowned by a true eucharistic commemoration. There was no such thing as a profane meal. This had already been true in the Jewish tradition. It was all the more so for Christians, since their Lord had eaten with them, especially at that Last Supper which he had invited them to renew forever afterwards "in memory of him." In every Christian meal, the thanksgiving and even perhaps the joy of taking food in common with the brethren must suggest an even deeper communion and a more efficacious Eucharist.

We must understand in this way, it seems, St. Paul's insistence on inviting the faithful to practice acts of thanksgiving and charity in all their meals (cf. 1 Cor. 10: 23-31; Rom. 14: 3f.; 1 Tim. 4: 3-4), and also the cordial as well as religious, if not specifically eucharistic atmosphere, of the meal he provided for his companions in shipwreck on his last journey to Rome (cf. Acts 27: 33-38). There are still families and Christian communities where one enjoys this brotherly, religious, and almost eucharistic atmosphere at every meal taken in common.

Paschal Meal to Paschal Sacrifice

Now that in charity, joy, and thanksgiving at the meal of the brethren, "the whole Church, from all parts of the earth, is assembled in thy kingdom" (Did. 9: 4), the action of the Christian mystery can be continued. Essentially eucharistic because the ancient promises begin to be fulfilled, the new Pasch is also essentially eschatological, that is, turned towards the future, and their perfect consummation. United in their common charity to Christ who presides over their paschal meal, the members of the People of God now can, and must, become part of him in the way that he indicates, just as the Hebrews of old united around Moses at the first Pasch and went with him into the desert of the Covenant.

What is the direction and what is this new desert of the New Covenant? The words pronounced by Jesus at the time when his disciples were receiving that bread and that wine no less than the circumstances in which he pronounced those words predicting his imminent death leave us convinced: It is the direction of Calvary; this is the desert of the Covenant in his blood. "And he took bread, and when he had given thanks he broke it and gave it to them, saying 'This is my body'" (Lk. 22: 19-20).

Here we have a profound aspect of our eucharistic Paschs. If, unlike the Jewish Pasch which began with a sacrifice, they begin, and must begin, in the fraternal joy of a communion in the Lord, whereby it is shown that they belong to the time of fulfilled promises in the blessing given to Abraham, they cannot stop there; they must continue the fraternal action even to the Calvary of Jesus, to the cross and the Covenant which alone can seal this fraternity. They must consummate in the blood of the Messiah that blessing of all the families of the earth. If Jesus wanted the eucharistic supper to come before his Passion and not, for instance, after his Resurrection, it is because the Messiah (head and members) and messianic people had to climb Calvary and offer there the messianic sacrifice in which the new and eternal messianic Covenant would be sealed.

One can see the difference that exists by way of preparation required between the Jewish and the Christian Pasch. In each case, the preparation is indispensable. If God in Egypt and if Jesus at the Last Supper and on Calvary took the initiative in the liberating Pasch, in each case the people of God had to actively prepare the Pasch. Exodus (chap. 12) and the synoptics (cf. Mt. 26: 17-19; Mk. 14: 12-16; Lk. 22: 7-13) insist on this preparation. The liturgy of the Mass also emphasizes its importance and asks all of us, ministers as well as faithful, to take an active part in it. But the preparations for the Christian Pasch, because of the inverting of the order of the meal and the sacrifice in comparison with the Jewish Pasch and because of the deeper mysteries involved in this Christian Pasch, are not concerned merely with the matter of the sacrifice or with the meal. Even more than the Jewish Pasch, the Christian one requires an active preparation of people, and this is done by their entering into the movement of fraternal communion, which we have seen to be essential to the Last Supper. As the Jews in their paschal tradition, the apostles had to prepare "at such a person's house" (Mt. 26: 18) all that was required by the rites, and Judas could also have taken part in this preparation. But in the course of the ritual development of the Jewish Pasch, Jesus taught his own by everything in his bearing as well as by explicit teaching that the preparation of the new Pasch had gone beyond the ritual order and that it consisted above all in the exercise of a fraternal charity that goes as far as that total communion of minds and hearts which the Last Supper inaugurated. This was a profound necessity not only because of the new Law (cf. Mt. 5: 23-24) but more especially because of that New Covenant in the blood of Jesus to which the new Pasch at the Last Supper began to introduce the whole People of God.

III

The Eucharist
as Paschal Sacrifice

The Institution of the Eucharist and the Passion

There is no doubt that the whole life of Jesus converged on his Passion which he looked upon as his hour in a very special way (cf. Mt. 16: 21; 17: 22; 20: 17-19; 26: 2; Jn. 2: 4; 7: 30; 8: 20; 13: 1) and there is still less doubt that he wanted to indicate the close relationship between that Passion and the Eucharist. These two facts are sufficiently attested to in the Gospels so that they need not be emphasized here. Everything in the eucharistic supper is directed to the Passion, and in some way introduces it—the ancient rites of the Jewish Pasch, the new rite of bread and wine, separately presented as the body and blood of the Lord and which would be separated on the following day, the words pronounced during the ceremony, the feeling and content of the farewell speech, and the departure for the Garden of Olives.

In the Pauline theology of the Eucharist as expressed in the First Epistle to the Corinthians as well as in the Johannine theology in Chapter 6 in his Gospel and

Epistles (cf. 1 Jn. 4: 9-12), the close relationship in each case is assumed as a basic fact. And if the Acts of the Apostles (cf. Acts 10: 41) and a few other ancient documents seem to bring out the relationship of the first eucharistic meals of the community and those that the risen Jesus took with his disciples, this relationship, far from contradicting the one that exists between the Eucharist and the Passion, presupposes it in an obvious way just as the Resurrection presupposes the Passion. It proves only that the relationship applies to the whole mystery, which includes without separation the Passion and the Resurrection. We shall return to this later.

The Death of Jesus in the History of the People of God

At this point in the study of the paschal mystery, one must give attention both to the exterior and apparent history of the People of God and to the more hidden mysteries which were fulfilled in Jesus. To arrive at an understanding of the latter, one must pass through the former. From the exterior point of view, the facts, however tragic they may be, amount to this: the rejection and crucifixion of the Messiah by the messianic people. Jesus is rejected by the People of God precisely when he was leading them into the time of the New Covenant and when he was giving it universal extension.

The Gospels bring this out clearly. In the final trial, the three societies which represent the People of God extended at this very moment to include all humanity speak up one after the other to condemn or reject the Messiah each in its own way. At that moment the Jewish people by recognizing their Messiah in Jesus, ought to have proclaimed to all the families of the earth the

realization of the universal promises which it had in-
herited for them. Jesus who yesterday and often before
had tried to gather Israel about him "as a hen gathers her
chickens under her wings" (Mt. 23: 37-39; Lk. 13: 34-
35) had to announce prophetically its dispossession in
favor of other nations of its promised inheritance (cf.
the allegory of the bad vinedressers: Mt. 21: 33-34; Mk.
12: 1-11; Lk. 20: 9-18). To the very end, however, he
showed that as far as he was concerned, he intended to
respect their privileges (cf. Mt. 10: 5-6; 15: 24) and this
last Pasch, unlike the preceding one (cf. Jn. 7:8; 7: 10)
he celebrated in public communion with the Jewish
people (cf. Mt. 26: 17-19). And yet, by the legitimate
organ of their synagogue in a case for which they had
competence and by the shouts of the crowd who preferred
Barabbas to Jesus, the Jewish people rejected their
Messiah.

Likewise, the temporal society represented by the
Roman Empire, to which Jesus in one of his very last
pronouncements (cf. Mt. 22: 15-22; Lk. 12:14) had
just given a foundation to last for all subsequent times
as a naturally autonomous power, condemned him to
death by the authority of Pilate and mocked him by the
deplorable behavior of the guards.

Lastly, the Church, the religious society of the future,
after having betrayed Jesus in the person of Judas, denies
him in Peter, its head, and abandons him to his solitude
in the other disciples. As the Pasch proceeds, the Church
itself could follow Jesus as far as the intimacy in the
Cenacle, but not as far as the death on the cross.

And so, at the very time when Jesus is accomplishing
the new Pasch which is to inaugurate the messianic times
and introduce the People of God into the New Covenant
this people as a whole turns away from him, according to

Isaiah's prophecy (cf. Is. 53: 37) and the great messianic Psalm (cf. Ps. 22: 7). He must face the great struggle of his Passion and death alone. Of course, near him on Calvary will be Mary, his mother, with John, his disciple, and a few other women; these few faithful ones share in the solitude of Jesus in the midst of his people, but do not eliminate it. As the mystery of the Passion proceeds, the People of God bring to it only the weight of their sins or their indifference, and Jesus alone bears the burden in presenting himself to his Father.

The death of Jesus, then, seems, first of all, to be a rejection of the Messiah by the qualified representatives of the messianic people. The fact that this rejection also included the corporal and moral torment of the Passion, and that it was sealed on the cross, adds nothing, however important it may be on the spiritual plane, nothing essential to the first statement. It was precisely when, through Jesus, they were entering into the messianic era of their universal extension and of the fulfillment of the promises made to Abraham that the People of God in the crowds as well as in their leaders committed their supreme infidelity and crucified the Messiah who, over and above this, happened to be the Son of God himself. More serious than the infidelity of Kadesh where the whole People of God apostatized and when Moses himself fell into sin, the death of Jesus seems at first, at the climax of the history of the People of God, to be the greatest iniquity of that people (cf. Mt. 21: 33-34; Mk. 12: 1-11; Lk. 20: 9-18). How did Jesus himself look at it?

Jesus Faces His Own Death

Jesus had explicitly foreseen and at the same time announced his death, and his Resurrection (cf. Mt. 16: 21; 17: 22; 20: 19; 26: 32; Mk. 14: 28; Jn. 2: 19). He had even distinguished the collective responsibilities that have just been mentioned: that of the elders, the scribes and priests for the Jewish people (cf. Mt. 16: 21; 20: 18), that of the pagans, that is, Romans (cf. Mt. 20: 18-19; 26: 2; Acts 2: 23), that of the disciples by the betrayal of Judas (cf. Mt. 26: 20-25; Mk. 14: 17-21; Lk. 22: 21-23; Gen. 13: 18-30), and the denial of Peter and the desertion of the rest (cf. Mt. 26: 31-35; Mk. 14: 26-31; Lk. 22: 31-34; Jn. 13: 36-38; 16: 32). But beyond these responsibilities that were immediate and apparent he had seen those of all men (cf. Mt. 17: 22; Mk. 9: 30; Lk. 9: 44) and more specifically those of all men inasmuch as they are sinners (cf. Mt. 26: 45; Mk. 14: 41). On the other hand, by insisting on calling the hour of his death his hour, the one for which he had come (cf. Mt. 26: 45; Mk. 14: 35; 14: 41; Jn. 12: 27; 17: 1), and by always referring to it as "necessary" (cf. Mt. 16: 21; Mk. 8: 31; Lk. 9: 22; 9: 44; 12: 50; Jn. 3: 14)—just as after his Resurrection he says: "it was necessary" (cf. Lk. 24: 26; 24: 44; 24: 46)—he clearly showed that he considered this death not as a crime of men but as required by an even deeper mystery that he alone grasped and which concerned the redemption of all men and the glory of his Father.

At the same time, it must be remembered that in those moments when he was revealing so clearly the foreknowledge of his death and those who were to blame for it, Jesus never evinced the slightest bitterness toward those who were responsible. The perfect holiness that his

Passion was to consummate, continued on to the end for their sake, he said (cf. Jn. 17: 19). In his attitude toward Judas (cf. Mt. 26: 50; Lk. 22: 48), the servants of the high priest (cf. Lk. 22: 51f.; Mt. 26: 55f.; Mk. 14: 48f.; Lk. 22: 42f.), the cowardly disciples when he was arrested (cf. Jn. 18: 8), Peter (cf. Lk. 22: 61-62), Caiphas (cf. Jn. 18: 20-21), the Sanhedrin (cf. Mt. 27: 11; Mk. 15: 2; Lk. 23: 3; Jn. 18: 33-38), or the Roman soldiers (cf. Mt. 27: 27f.; Mk. 15: 16-19; Jn. 19: 2-3), Jesus preserves in every case, even in the most painful hours of his Passion, his unalterable kindness, patient with all, pardoning all and finally pleading before his Father their ignorance of the mystery involved in his death, which we shall soon see was the mystery of redemption (cf. Lk. 23: 34). This simultaneity and this contrast of the universal responsibility for the death of Jesus and of the unalterable and universal mercifulness of Jesus for men at the very heart of his Passion are essential to the mystery which is accomplished. Toward this as the consequence of the Pasch we are proceeding step by step.

There is, however, another aspect to the mystery which Jesus used to insist on when he spoke of his approaching death. He saw this death essentially as a combat. It was not so much a combat with men: The human actors in this drama would take part in it, we repeat, more out of ignorance than malice and because of this, Jesus would argue to obtain for men, by his very death, the mercy of his Father (cf. Lk. 23: 34). It was rather a combat with Satan (cf. Lk. 22: 31), the prince of this world (cf. Jn. 12: 31; 14: 30; 16: 11; 2 Cor. 4: 4; Eph. 2: 2), whose hour, the hour of the powers of darkness (cf. Lk. 22: 53), was mingled with that of Jesus. Of this combat, the outcome, according to Jesus,

was not in doubt: the strong one would be put in chains
and dispossessed by the stronger one (cf. Lk. 11: 21-22).
Satan would be cast out (cf. Jn. 14: 30) and would
submit to judgment (cf. Jn. 16: 11) while Jesus, by that
death in which Satan had thought to conquer, would
triumph over him and thereafter would irresistibly
attract all things to himself (cf. Jn. 12: 32). His triumph
in his Resurrection and his glorious return to his Father
would begin to prove this (cf. Jn. 17: 1f.). It is precisely
by this combat and this victory that the true Joshua
would have the whole People of God pass into the true
land of promise and the definitive Covenant. The new
Pasch, by uniting the whole people in communion with
this combat and this victory of their head, would also
cause them to effect this great passage.

To one who thus approaches the Passion and death of
Jesus from the outside by simply following the account
of the facts in this last Pasch, Jesus appears to have the
sovereign mastery of an unconquerable warrior. "No one
takes my life, but I lay it down of my own accord. I have
power to lay it down, and I have power to take it again;
this charge I have received from my Father" (Jn. 10:
18). When one goes back over the detailed episodes of
the Passion and looks over the whole series of renounce-
ments that Jesus meets with from the most external to
the most intimate and mysterious, he finds everywhere,
on the one hand, the supreme liberty with which he faces
them, the victorious mastery with which he enters and
goes through with them, and, on the other hand, as the
soul of this liberty, as the secret of this mastery, he sees
a great love for men and a clear and complete conformity
of his will with the wishes of his Father. Through this
liberty and charity we must now penetrate even deeper

into the mystery of the new Pasch. For this we must set the facts back in their paschal perspective.

The Paschal Immolation of Calvary

By attracting attention during the Last Supper to the bread and wine and by presenting them separately as his body "delivered for you" and as his blood "shed for you," Jesus not only pointed out the relation of the new rite to the death he was to undergo shortly afterwards on Calvary but also suggested that henceforth, this death would take the place of the paschal sacrifice with which the new Pasch allows us to enter into communion. He invited us to see the reality and mystery of his own death through the figurative teaching of the Paschal immolation of the Exodus, with those reservations required by the transfer in substituting real time for figurative time. Just as in Egypt the blood of the sacrificed lamb had preserved the Hebrews from the avenging passage of Yahweh, and just as the flesh of the lamb had nourished them for their passage through the desert to the Covenant and the promised land, the flesh and blood of Jesus consumed under the species of eucharistic bread and wine, would nourish the messianic people in their progress through the desert of this world toward the lasting Covenant and the definitive promises. It would, above all, preserve them from the punishments deserved by their faults. That Jesus had previously and explicitly attributed to his death the value of a redemptive immolation, the texts do not allow us to doubt. "The Son of man," he said, "came not to be served but to serve, and to give his life as a ransom for many" (Mt. 20: 28; cf. Mk. 10: 45). Likewise, when he declared during the Last Supper, "The

Son of man goes as it is written of him, but woe to that man by whom the Son of man is betrayed! It would have been better for that man if he had not been born" (Mt. 26: 24; cf. Mk. 14: 21; Lk. 22: 22), or when, giving himself as an example, he assures his disciples that "Greater love has no man than this, that a man lay down his life for his friends" (Jn. 15: 13), he is undoubtedly referring to the great messianic texts which foretold the sufferings and death of the Messiah, and their redemptive value (cf. Ps. 22; Is. 53; Dan. 9: 25f.). The prophecy of *Isaiah* especially brings out in the death of the Messiah the two aspects which the sacrifice of the paschal lamb had included: the appeasement of justice and the divine vengeance for the sins of the people, (cf. Is. 53: 4-5; 53: 6, 8, 10; Exod. 12: 12, 13, 23, 27, 29; Num. 33: 4), and the efficacy of this ransom for the liberation of the people (cf. Is. 53: 5, 10, 11). Unquestionably, it was in this perspective that Jesus looked at his death. When St. Paul develops his theology of the redemption along these lines, he is not innovating; he is simply being faithful to the explicit teaching of Jesus himself (cf. Rom. 4: 25; 1 Cor. 25: 4; 2 Cor. 5: 21; Gal. 3: 13-14; Heb. 9: 28).

God's Will to Save All Men

How did the shedding of Jesus' blood on the cross obtain the value of sacrifice, of paschal immolation for the People of God in messianic times? It is all the more important to know that with the order of the meal and immolation reversed in respect to the order in the Exodus, all the members of the messianic people participating in the new Pasch found themselves invited by the progress of this Pasch to pass from the meal to the immolation, to follow Jesus from the supper to Calvary. They were invited to prolong their fraternal communion around Jesus in a communion that was as complete as possible in the mystery of his Passion, and Resurrection.

Now having asked the question, it is obvious that the answer must be sought in the soul of Jesus and not solely in the somewhat material elements of his sacrifice. "It is the spirit that gives life, the flesh is of no avail; the words that I have spoken to you are spirit and life" (Jn. 6: 63), he had said himself in his teaching on the bread of life when he had proclaimed that one could not have life if one did not eat his flesh and drink his blood. This amounted to saying that eating his flesh and drinking his blood necessarily entailed sharing in the life that animated them. This life was that of the soul of Jesus at the time when he was sacrificing his flesh and his blood in his Passion. The perfection of the sacrifices of the old Law lay in the exact performance of external rites. By contrast, the perfection of this sacrifice consists, first of all, in the soul itself of the one who consummates it, in what the Epistle to the Hebrews refers to as the "eternal spirit" of Jesus (Heb. 9: 14). One thinks of the version in the Septaugint of Psalm 40, verses 6 and 7, and of the commentary on them in the same Epistle to the Hebrews: "Then I said, 'Lo, I come; in the roll of the book it is written of me; I delight to do thy will, O my God; thy law is within my heart' " (Ps. 40: 7-8; cf. Heb. 10: 5f.).

The will of God is the very foundation of the mystery of the immolation of Jesus. We have begun to glimpse the most obvious characteristics of the spirit of the Savior in this immolation: absolute liberty and perfect interior control, unwavering love for men and endless mercy for all their crimes including the one that they have just now been guilty of toward him, and the clear foreknowledge and willed acceptance of his suffering and death. From here, one must go even deeper to reach the depths and the soul of all the rest, namely, total obedience to what Jesus esteems to be the will of his Father. No doubt, this was always the most characteristic and the most constant trait of his psychology as it is shown to us in the Gospels. From the first words of his childhood that are known and in which he asserts the duty, above all else, of attending to the affairs of his Father (cf. Lk. 2: 49) until the days of his Passion, he always lived in the strictest and most conscious dependence on the will of his Father. "My food," he said, "is to do the will of him who sent me, and to accomplish his work" (Jn. 4: 34). And again, "I can do nothing on my own authority, as I hear, I judge; and my judgment is just, because I seek not my own will but the will of him who sent me" (Jn. 5: 30). And here at the end of his life and at the height of his suffering in the Passion, whether during the agony in the garden (cf. Mk. 14: 32-42), or at the last word reported by St. Luke (cf. Lk. 23: 46), it is obvious his deliberate strength of purpose more than ever relies on the will of God. Accepting the struggle with the powers of darkness, loving the sinful men whom the successful combat gives him power over— all this is primarily for Jesus accepting and fulfilling the will of his Father.

This is important, for there are not for Jesus—nor for us if we understand properly—two loves, one for men and one for his Father. It is in loving men that he conforms to the will of his Father whom he loves. The will of the Father, the work that it commands him to do (cf. Jn. 4: 34), has always been presented by Jesus as the salvation of men, and their salvation is the object of his own mission. "So it is not the will of my Father who is in heaven that one of these little ones should perish" (Mt. 18: 14), and again: "All that the Father gives me will come to me; and him who comes to me I will not cast out. For I have come down from heaven, not to do my own will, but the will of him who sent me; and this is the will of him who sent me, that I should lose nothing of all that he has given me, but raise it up at the last day. For this is the will of my Father, that every one who sees the Son and believes in him should have eternal life; and I will raise him up at the last day" (Jn. 6: 37-40). In the same speech on the bread of life, he had already explained, in view of this fulfilling of the will of the Father, what a close connection would exist between the three spiritual moments, as it were, of the new Pasch: the bread and wine of the fraternal meal that was to be substituted for the meal of the Jewish Pasch, his Passion and death which the bread and wine would give the power to communicate, and lastly, the will of the Father which was to be concurred in during the first two stages and which consisted of assuring sinful men of eternal life and resurrection. So true is this that for Jesus, willing the institution of the Eucharist, willing his Passion and death, and willing salvation and eternal life for all men amounted to one single will, which coincided exactly with the will of his Father who is in heaven. By his freely willed immolation on Calvary, and by the sharing in it that he gave us in the mystery of the Eucharist, he was consciously and simultaneously freeing the people of God from the slavery of sin and from the grasp of the devil more effectively than the paschal lamb had freed the Hebrews. He was aware of fulfilling completely by the same act the will of God in the new and eternal Covenant.

The New Covenant in Christ's Blood

On Calvary, in the act of Christ's accomplishing the will of his Father, he shed his blood for the salvation of men, and in his words at the Last Supper he established the new and eternal Covenant. In this act, the transition is made from the figurative order to that of reality. To the first belongs the shedding of blood. Every covenant in the old Law was concluded according to a ritual of blood; some of the blood was offered to God on the altar and the rest scattered over his people (cf. Exod. 24: 4-8; cf. Mt. 27: 25: "His blood be on us and on our children!"). To the second, inseparable from the first, belongs the charity of Christ himself offering the blood of the New Covenant. Hence it is on that act of charity of Christ on the cross that the whole mystery of the Pasch converges.

To penetrate more deeply into the understanding of this act, it is necessary to guard against a sort of adoptionism which unduly confuses the mystery of this act and that of the Incarnation, or the hypostatic union. Secondly, one must see plainly how this act is merely the inauguration for the people of God of the new and eternal Covenant.

It will not be necessary to dwell on the first point. Even if the Church had not clearly defined that the hypostatic union of the Word and the sacred humanity took place at the first moment of the virginal conception of Mary, the Gospel texts would prove sufficiently that Jesus' personally belonging to the transcendent and divine order did not begin with the Passion. Even at the baptism in the Jordan, the Father manifested his total, and one might say, his anterior delight in the one whom he wished his people to recognize as his own Son (cf.

Mt. 3: 17; Mk. 1: 11; Lk. 3: 22). At the time of the transfiguration a similar theophany gave the same testimony (cf. Mt. 17: 5; Mk. 9: 35; 2 Peter 1: 17). In his teaching, Jesus himself had often affirmed, independently of his Passion, his mysterious belonging by right of birth to the divine order. His whole conduct had multiplied proofs of this belonging.

And yet in many ways, especially when he spoke of his Passion and called it his hour, Jesus made one think that if the mystery of his Person were independent of his Passion, the mystery of his mission in the People of God was carried out only by this. The texts invite us to think that in the unfolding of the divine economy, the two mysteries were ordered to each other, and that the Incarnation of the Word in Jesus had as its end that act of charity from the height of the cross in which the whole work of Jesus was summed up. In any case, it was by this act itself, and not directly by the preparations that were required of the Messiah who was to accomplish it that God willed to conclude for all time between himself and his people the new and eternal Covenant. It was toward the act, not toward its preparation that the ancient types converged. Before the suffering and death of Jesus, the union in his Person of the divinity and the humanity, the union consummated at the first instant of his virginal conception was of interest only to his sacred humanity. It did not begin to interest the People of God, that is, all men, until Jesus performed on Calvary that act of charity to which the whole mystery of his life was leading. That is why all the new Pasch also had to converge entirely on that act.

What can we understand about this act? As we were saying, it is precisely in this act that the transition is made from the order of type and figure (the preparation) to the order of reality (the consummation). In considering the mysteries proper to the latter, one cannot remain excessively dependent on aspects which only apply to the former. In the literature concerning the eucharistic mystery or the sacrifice of the cross, discussion of either one by considering the sacrifices and worship of the old Law (as one should) may give great emphasis to the religious value without always noticing sufficiently that in essentials this sacrifice and this Eucharist are now of a different order—the order of charity. Certainly, the order of charity, particularly by the obedience to the will of God involved in it, satisfies to an eminent degree all the exigencies in the order of religion. Still, it goes well beyond it to the same degree that the New Covenant surpasses the old, or in other words, as much as figure is surpassed by reality, accomplishment by promises, and expectation by possession. Only the order of charity, not that that of religion, could give such reality, accomplishment, and possession. The new Pasch is necessarily a Pasch of charity. To understand this more clearly, we must now consider charity and its truly divine mysteries.

The New Covenant in the Holy Spirit

We now cross over into a new and important phase of the Pasch. Hitherto, we have considered the charity of Christ on the cross in the perspective of its content, or its objects: all men and, inseparably, the will of the Father. Going further, we must now find the source. If the act by which Christ on the cross sacrifices himself for all men in obedience to the will of his Father is the greatest act of charity not only of his life but of all the acts that have ever issued from created liberty (by reason of the divine mystery of his person), then it is the fruit at one and the same time of his most free human will and of an incomparable communication of this will to the mystery of the God-charity. This is what is presently in need of emphasis.

If it is true indeed that "hope does not disappoint us, because God's love has been poured into our hearts through the Holy Spirit which has been given to us" (Rom. 5: 5), the Holy Spirit must have flowed abundantly into the soul of Christ to produce the act of the fullness of that act of charity accomplished at the height of the cross. We have already seen the immensity of this act for all men and for his Father, but have considered it in its created aspect only. Seen from its uncreated aspect, it now appears primarily as the fruit in Jesus, Son of the Father, not only of the fullness of the gift of the Holy Spirit but also, in view of its content from the very beginning, as the love for the men whom he must save, as the manifestation of an infinite love for men, the source of which is in God himself, and which is communicated to men in Jesus. At the climax of the history and mystery of the People of God we find an act in which the eternal and infinite love that God has for men erupts into history and into creation. The same act is Jesus sacrificing himself for all men in fulfilling the will of his Father. Since the love of Jesus consists essentially in sacrificing everything that he can sacrifice, even his life, it must be said that it is first of all in God that such a love for men is found which goes to the extent of sacrificing for them the Son of God himself. This is a very great mystery, and yet scripture teaches it to us explicitly: "For God so loved the world that he gave his only Son, that whoever believes in him should not perish but have eternal life" (Jn. 3: 16). "He who did not spare his own Son but gave him up for us all, will he not also give us all things with him?" (Rom. 8: 32). Infinite love did just that.

The Sacrifice of Abraham and the Sacrifice of the Father

At this point, the sacrifice of Christ, the mystery of the voluntary sacrifice of the Son by the Father, must be seen from the perspective of another immolation of a son by his father, the sacrifice of Abraham. This gives to the mystery of the People of God its profound meaning and import. Between the sacrifice during the typological and pedagogical preparation, the time of Abraham, and the real sacrifice of the latter days, that of the Son of God on Calvary, there is a double relationship. First of all, just as in the holocaust that Abraham agreed to make of "his only son, the one whom he loved, Isaac" (Gen. 22: 2), the Father of the People of God had given a testimony of the absolute right of God that was as complete as it could be, since he did not hesitate to sacrifice to him the whole future and existence of that people (cf. Gen. 22: 12). In the same way, the absolute mystery of God as love finds its striking manifestation in the immolation that he makes of his own Son in creation for the salvation of men (cf. Jn. 3: 16; Rom. 5: 8; 8: 32). And this manifestation outside the infinite love which is in God seems to be the ultimate reason for this creation, crowned by the Passion of the Son of God: This is why when approaching his Passion, the Lord finds in it a source of glory for himself and a glory like that which is found eternally with his Father in eternity (Jn. 17: 2-5). From the Passion of Christ stems for God the greatest glory in creation.

On the other hand, the immediate fruit of the holocaust of Abraham was the solemn and definitive pronouncement of the divine promise that his posterity would be as numerous as the stars in the heavens and the sands by the sea, that it would triumph over all its enemies, and that in it all the families of the earth would be blessed (cf. Gen. 22: 15-18). So likewise, the immediate and necessary fruit of Christ's holocaust of love on the cross can be none other than the fulfillment of these promises in a new and eternal Covenant. In other words, it means the actual extending of the blessing and salvation of God to all the families of the earth, the communicating to the People of God identified henceforth with all humanity of the strength of God himself in its fight against its invisible enemies and the growth of his people into a multitude as numerous as the stars of heaven or the sands of the sea (cf. Mt. 18: 14; 1 Tim. 2: 4; 4: 10).

The Sacrifice of Abraham, the Sacrifice of the Pasch, the Sacrifice of Jesus

If the sacrifice of Christ on the cross is properly looked upon, first of all, in the perspective of the paschal immolation, one is inevitably led, because of its very origin, to look upon it in the wider perspective of the promises. The gratuitous period of the promises made to Abraham and the contractual period of the paschal Covenant made with Moses merge at this point. Their unequal directions unite in that act on the cross when the man in Jesus gives everything to God and when Jesus bursts into creation by his sacrifice of love to display that infinite mystery of love, which is God. God in Jesus gives to his people, to all men, pardon, first of all, for the infidelities committed during the contractual period of the first Covenant (cf. Heb. 9: 15), and second, the plenary gift of the true object of the promises, himself. The two great sacrifices of the period of types and preparation, that is, the holocaust by Abraham that introduced the period of gratuitous promises, and the paschal immolation that introduced the contractual period of the Covenant, now give place not only figuratively but actually to that sacrifice in which until the end of time, the universal people of God will find their continuous liberation from sinful enslavement and the beginning of the enjoyment of God's free gifts.

It is readily understood that the People of God had to be led to this point by the new Pasch. Only in the overall charity of Christ's sacrifices could those three elements be found without which they would cease to be God's people. Their inner solidarity in charity, initiated imperfectly (as was seen at the Last Supper) in the fraternal meal of the new Pasch, can only be consummated and permanently cemented by association with the charity of Christ for all men, which goes as far as the sacrifice and which stems from the total gift of the Holy Spirit (cf. 1 Jn. 3: 16). There is a liberation from sin and a domination over the powers of evil: Jesus Christ is the only one over whom neither the devil nor sin have power (cf. Jn. 14: 30; 2 Cor. 5: 21; Heb. 7: 26; 1 Jn. 3: 5), and the People of God triumph over the devil only in the strength and holiness of his victory (cf. Jn. 17: 19; Rom. 8: 1f.; Heb. 10: 10). Finally they enter into possession of the divine heritage. Only through charity and communion with the Holy Spirit can the full mystery of God be communicated to the People of God. In short, in the charity of Christ on the cross imparted by the new Pasch, the People of God find at the same time total liberation from all enslavement as the Mosaic Pasch had prefigured and that supernatural blessing and universal expansion which had been foretold them by the divine promises through Abraham.

The Triumphant Pasch

Because the new Pasch necessarily leads those who expose themselves to its movement as far as the act of Christ's charity, it could not be other than triumphant. It not only prepares for the Covenant as the Pasch of Exodus did, but it leads to it by its whole intent. It is that same new and eternal Covenant—new like the Messiah who inaugurates it, eternal like the charity that "never passes away" (1 Cor. 13: 8) and like the Holy Spirit who is given thereby in all the plenitude of his gifts. It is the triumphant Pasch of Jesus, first of all, the messianic leader of the people, and then of the members of his body, who are the People of God, his Church.

In what concerns the Savior, the victory of course does not begin only at his Resurrection. His victory is, first of all, that act of charity from the height of the cross in which he inaugurated with his Father in the Holy Spirit the new and eternal Covenant. In this act his love for his Father and for men triumphs over hatred and indifference in the world; in this act his complete fidelity to the will of his Father overcomes the natural anguish of his created will faced with suffering and death (cf. Mt. 26: 37f.). His victory is won by his willed emptying of himself. His victory is the mystery of his *kenosis* (cf. Phil. 2: 7). Let us remain true on this essential point to the only authentic Christian tradition, namely, that which considers the cross more as the image of the real triumph of Christ than as that of his apparent defeat. On this point Byzantine iconography is truer and less threatening to the faith of the simple than Western iconography, which comes from primitives, usually underlines the agony and suffering of the crucified and reserves the expression of his triumph to pictures of his Resurrection. Christ triumphs on the cross, and this triumph starts with that act whereby, going to the very end to death in his love for men and for his Father, he joins and makes his own the gift that his Father made to him in the Holy Spirit, for himself and for men—the fullness of life.

His sacred humanity is the first to receive the benefits of this fullness of life as shown outwardly by the Resurrection and Ascension. But through this glorious humanity of the Savior and beyond it, the people of God and all creation are drawn into the irresistible path of this victory. Jesus had foreseen it and his first witnesses will live in the enthusiasm of this victory which has become theirs. "... and I, when I am lifted up from the earth, will draw all men to myself" (Jn. 12: 32). He says after the Resurrection: "All authority in heaven and on earth has been given to me" (Mt. 28: 18). St. Paul is referring to this when, after describing the willed self-emptying of him who was in the form of God; he goes on to say: "... that at the name of Jesus every knee should bow, in heaven and on earth and under the earth, and every tongue confess that Jesus Christ is Lord, to the glory of God the Father" (Phil. 2: 9-11).

But it is not only for himself and in himself that Jesus triumphs, any more than it is in himself and for himself alone that he has struggled. "For them do I sanctify myself," he said (Jn. 17: 19). He triumphs also for them and in them, that is, for his people and in his people. "I have said this to you, that in me you may have peace. In the world you have tribulation; but be of good cheer. I have overcome the world" (Jn. 16: 33). From the day of Pentecost when he began to animate his Church by the breath of his victory—"it is the Spirit that gives life" (Jn. 6: 63)—until the final burst of the glorious Parousia, the latter days are, the time of the irresistible extension of his victory, that victory of the immolated lamb of which St. John in the Apocalypse has shown us the stages and variations.

The triumphant character is essential to the new Pasch, by which the People of God never ceases to approach that act of Christ's charity on the cross when the total gift was made to men. For the People of God, until the Parousia, every Pasch will have to be primarily a Pasch involving the road to Calvary, even a crucifying Pasch. All those who enter upon it, especially those who lend themselves to the redemptive demands of fraternal charity that become more and more universal in the eucharistic banquet, will be drawn into following the Savior as far as possible on the road to Calvary carrying their crosses (cf. Mt. 16: 24). In the measure of their grace they will be obliged perhaps to go very far in this direction, to the very foot of the cross where Mary and a few faithful ones are standing actively occupied by the mystery that is accomplished there by her Son (cf. Jn. 19: 25). Until the end of time apostles will be needed to make up what is wanting to the sufferings of Christ in their flesh, for his body which is the Church (Col. 1: 24). The Eucharist, for those who receive it, will always be presenting deeper and more universal demands. At the same time, it must not be forgotten that it is truly a triumphant Pasch as a crucifying Pasch. To the degree that they lend themselves to its action, they will enter into the total and immense victory of Christ; they will make this victory theirs and extend it. In this participation, which they find in the Passion of Christ, they will rejoice (cf. Col. 1: 24; Rom. 5: 3-4; Phil. 2: 17; 2 Cor. 7: 4); the strength that they find in the Pasch will be none other than the strength of the risen Christ, and even more than that. It will be the strength of the vivifying Spirit which the crucified Christ won for them on the cross and which had its first visible manifestation for us in the Resurrection of Jesus. By this Pasch the same vivifying Spirit in them as in Jesus will tend to bring about not only the future resurrection of their bodies but also and first of all, as a prerequisite of their resurrection, the justification and sanctification of their souls.

The Eucharistic Pasch

Therefore, the new Pasch is truly and thoroughly eucharistic, that is, overflowing with thanksgiving. This is true because by its very origin, it never ceases to initiate the messianic time of fulfilled promises for the People of God. This is also true in its final end because Jesus, who inaugurated the Pasch, has already gone in person to the consummation of that mystery and because he triumphs for ever in heaven where at the right hand of the Father, he never ceases to attract irresistibly his whole people. Lastly, this is true even in the process since it is in this irresistible strength of Christ and therefore victoriously that those members struggle here below for the consummation of the mystery of the Church. From one end to the other, it is the same triumph that the People of God are to proclaim in their thanksgiving. And as for the few who are already liberated from the idolatrous slavery of Egypt, but are still struggling in the austerity of the desert before reaching in their turn the splendors of the promised land, their triumph will be all the more assured and thanksgiving will pour forth all the better from their hearts to the degree that they have clearly grasped the astonishing reality of that paschal mystery in which they are involved. This is the last stage of their journey.

IV

The Relevance of
the Eucharistic Pasch

The Relevance in the Words of Institution

When the Lord, for the profound reasons that we have tried to glimpse, willed to have his Church by the new Pasch enter into the new and eternal Covenant of the Holy Spirit in his blood, he was not satisfied with asking it to enter into his Passion by faith, by fraternal charity and by the acceptance of the Father's will. He took bread and said: "Take and eat, this is my body." He also took a cup of wine and said: "Drink, all, of this: it is my blood in the new covenant" (Mt. 26: 26-27). Neither the communion of faith nor the communion of charity with the People of God and with the mystery of the Passion are sufficient here, although they are indispensable; they must be reinforced and find all their relevance in the consuming of bread and wine, which the Lord presents as being really his body and blood sacrificed on the cross. Already the great discourse on the bread of life, reported by St. John (cf. Jn. 6), a speech that had shocked the Jews by its very relevance, had testified beyond a doubt in favor of this realism.

It is well known that Zwingli and Calvin, and following them the greater number of the Protestant Churches, believe that the Lord's words must be understood in a symbolic sense and deny their relevance. (Luther, himself, less influenced by the first enthusiasms of literary criticism than Zwingli and perhaps Calvin, denied this.) One contemporary bible, as useful as the protestant edition of Segond's translation (Paris, 1942) is careful to give many references, but in regard to the words of institution (Mt. 26: 26), it only refers to biblical texts where the copulative verb "is" is used in all possible literary senses (a parable: Mt. 13: 38-39; the explanation of a prophetic dream: Gen. 40: 12-13; an allegory: 1 Cor. 10: 4; an apocalyptic image: Rev. 1: 20), and excludes all those where it has the more natural and obvious affirmation of being.

The Church saw in this interpretation a great impoverishment of the patrimony confided to it and, in 1551 at the Council of Trent (Sess. XIII, Cap. 1 and Can. 1-4), authoritatively put forward in opposition the traditional realistic interpretation, even canonizing, as the Fourth Council of the Lateran (1215) had already done, the term "transubstantiation," which was used to describe it in the schools. Still earlier at the Roman Council of 1079 against Berengarius of Tours, it solemnly declared that "by the words of our Redeemer, the bread and wine on the altar are substantially changed into the true, proper and living flesh and blood of Jesus Christ our Lord." There is no doubt but what this is the sense in which the whole Christian tradition, except for a very few dissenters, has always understood the words of the eucharistic institution.

Faithful to the method required by our pastoral intent, we shall not go further into this controversy than the scholastic discussions connected with it. In line with the present essay, we shall point out that the purely symbolic interpretation, easy to accept at first, proves to be counter to the whole paschal mystery as we have envisaged it, and must be set aside at once for this very reason. We now begin to see clearly the full extent of the relevance of the eucharistic mystery.

At first sight one can understand why certain exegetes have hesitated to accept this interpretation of Jesus' words at the Last Supper, even though it is the most obvious. Nothing in the Old Testament and, strangely enough, nothing in the texts concerning the Pasch foreshadowed a new Pasch instituted with such relevance. The messianic prophecies that are most explicit certainly referred to the suffering and death of the servant of Yahweh, but they said nothing of the new Pasch that would be instituted before his death. It is, strictly speaking, possible that because of their biblical training, the apostles recognized in the Last Supper the new rite added by their master, in a not unusual way, to the extended paschal rites and linked them with the offering of Melchizedek; it is not impossible, by the same token, that they recognized these ancient rites as preparing and prefiguring this new mystery. What is certain is that, even if this is true the relevance of Jesus' words in instituting this mystery was something utterly new, which surpassed all the prefiguration. This affirmation of being belonged to a different climate from the symbolic rites and words of the Old Testament. It lead into a new world, as it were, a new order of things without precedent.

Consequently, the Reformers were justified to a certain extent when in keeping with the tendencies of a period which gave more attention to the literal meaning of the biblical texts than to the historical process which these texts revealed in the mystery of God's people, they were reluctant to admit the realism of the words of institution. A person who is accustomed to understand the New Testament in continuity with the images of the Old finds that Jesus' initiative at the Last Supper seems at first unexpected and novel, and hence unbelievable, if one understands the words in their most natural and relevant way.

But, when one thinks more about it and especially when one has grasped the importance in the divine economy as revealed in the Jewish and Christian revelation of the sequence of events as we mentioned in the beginning, it is precisely this novelty that pleads most convincingly in favor of the relevance of the Lord's words as well as the whole mystery of the new Pasch which they instituted. In fact, the case of the Eucharist is not unique in this. It verifies a law which is common to all aspects of the great messianic mystery. This law could be formulated as follows: In every messianic reality, two aspects may be discerned. By the first, which still belongs to history and its order of phenomena, this reality seems to be a continuity of the whole Old Testament and the terminus of its preparations and prefigurations. By the second, which escapes from the order of phenomena and transcends history, it seems, on the contrary, to be a new thing having nothing in common with the preparatory and prefiguring order. By the first, it enters into the continuity of figures. By the second, it goes beyond them and leads into the possession of the realities. By the first, that of its messianism, it is rooted in time and duration to bring them to their term. By the second, that of the Incarnation, it draws up out of time into eternity all that which eternity took over from the first.

If we take one by one all the values of the Old Testament which are gathered up and fulfilled by the messianic mystery, we can verify this law. The divine blessing on all the families of the land promised to Abraham to be carried out in the messianic future could certainly suggest the universalism and moral sanctity of Jesus' teaching and at the same time, strengthen it by his prophetic witness; it could not let us suspect that this sanctity would be a real participation in God's holiness nor hint that this universalism would rest on the relevance of the communion of saints, of the body of Christ "which is the Church" and finally on the Holy Spirit.

The Mosaic law, of course, could hope for its fulfillment in the new Law and not its suppression. Moreover, it would seem to be a providential preparation for the latter; it could not foreshadow the fraternal charity, of which the new law essentially consists and which would be, in the People of God, the very communication of the Holy Spirit of God.

Finally, just as in all these values which are solidly biblical and essentially messianic in the Old Covenant—the kingdom of God, redemption or liberation, a new heaven and a new earth—there is always some continuity and some ascent to a higher level, thus, marking the passage from types and figures to the order of reality and eternity.

The major case would obviously be that of the Messiah himself. The messianic prophecies could certainly foretell that he would effect the universal extension of the People of God in messianic times, that he would redeem his people by his suffering and death, and that in all this he would be in a singular proximity with God and under the incomparable influence of the Holy Spirit (cf. the Emmanuel of Isaiah). All these things do, in fact, appear in the Gospel, but they could not hint that this Messiah would be the Son of God himself in the eternity of the trinitarian mystery, that his Passion and his cross would be the ultimate explanation of the mystery of evil, and that all of humanity would subsist in his mysterious Person as his body.

This is what happens in the eucharistic Pasch. That it was prefigured and prepared in the time preceding the Messiah has been shown. On the other hand, one cannot deny that it is very obviously attached to these preparations and prefigurations and closely linked to the historical context in which it was instituted. But to say that the figurative words and gestures to which it is attached contain the whole reality is to deny that it belongs to messianic times and really enters upon the supratemporal and divine mysteries which characterize these times. If there is still a Pasch in messianic times, or the last days— and who could doubt it on seeing the acts and teaching of the Lord in the Gospel—this Pasch is nothing less than a participation in the divine reality of the whole messianic mystery. This is what leads us to understand the words by which Christ instituted the eucharistic Pasch in their most obvious meaning.

But at the same time, as we approach this higher level, we must try to glimpse what the realism of the new paschal mystery is.

The Relevance of the New Pasch

We have seen, through the teachings of the figurative period, how essential it is that the Pasch be a movement, a passage, a crossing over. A movement

toward the promised land and beyond, though uncon-
scious at first, toward the messianic era in which the last
promises are fulfilled: This is the Pasch of the Exodus.
A movement toward the New Covenant in the blood of
Jesus and in the Holy Spirit: This is the messianic Pasch
inaugurated at the Last Supper. To determine the nature
of each Pasch the end of each must be considered since
any movement is defined by its end.

The end of the Pasch of the Exodus was first the land
of Canaan, that is, a reality in time and space. The
Pasch, then, had caused a movement, a migration. We
have seen that, at least as a basis for its symbolism, this
geographic migration was central in the annual commemoration by the Jews of the first Pasch. Whether it
only reminded them of the past or whether even then, in
the sense explained above, it appeared as heralding the
future, the Jewish Pasch focused on the land of Canaan
and always looked upon it as the promised land. But if
a few more fervent Jews looking beyond the level of the
first promises and linking them with the promised blessing of Abraham's universal descendants, already saw
the spiritual movement in their annual Paschs, it is still
true that the former was necessary to reach the latter,
and even in the old days the paschal movement has as
its immediate end and first object the promised Land.
They could never reach the reality without passing
through the figures, which turn out to be entirely within
space and time.

On the contrary, with regard to its term, the New
Covenant with God in the blood of Jesus and in the Holy
Spirit, and with regard to the words of its institution,
"This *is* my body, this *is* my blood," the Pasch inaugur-
ated at the Last Supper from the beginning places its
term on a level which is no longer in space and time.

Even though the land of Canaan should enlarge its boundaries to include the whole earth, it is not by the promise of a land that the New Covenant between God and his people is established. Likewise, if the bread and wine "are" the body and blood of the Lord, it is clear that on the level of appearances and according to these the bread and wine (the body and blood) still belong to the order of space and time. If it had been on this level that the Lord in the new Pasch had willed to establish a relationship, a "passing over," from bread to his body, and from wine to his blood, he would have spoken of becoming and would have said, "This becomes my body, this becomes my blood." That is not what he said, and obviously, on the level of appearances, level of space and time, that is not what was produced nor what is now produced. On the level of appearances, in the order of space and time, the bread remains bread and the wine remains wine. If Jesus insists, "This is," it is because the mystery is accomplished on a deeper level of being where there is no becoming. However, since it is still a question of a Pasch, hence of a "passing over," it is also on this deeper level of being, of existence, that one must seek its end and nature. Once more, we come to the reality of all that belongs properly to the last times, and more must be said about this.

The Result of Transubstantiation

Certainly we are here discussing a mystery, and it is easily understood why the Christian doctors have studied it very cautiously and even awkwardly. The angle from which we approach it allows us to admire how faithful Christian tradition has been to the paschal perspective in which it was revealed to us, when it refused all explanations tending to locate in the bread and wine, and not in the body and blood, the term of the relationship expressed and effected by the Lord's word between the bread and wine on the one hand, and the body and blood on the other. Any eucharistic teaching which reverts, more or less, to that of impanation or of consubstantiation, or, any teaching of the real presence that suggests somehow a localization of the body and blood of the Lord in our measurable space, even supposing that it were understandable, errs already in that it violently inverts, as it were, the basic orientation of the paschal mystery. Such teachings reduce to the order of space and time that which is meant to draw us out of it. They suggest to the imagination some sort of return to earth on the part of Christ instead of telling us how to meet him by faith in heaven.

It is not certain whether some modern forms of devotion to the Eucharist have sufficiently respected the basic paschal orientation of its mystery. How many hymns make the faithful sing of descent on the altar or of his captivity in the tabernacle and thus, center the regard of faith here below in the very mystery that was meant to make them pass over into heaven. This is like saying to the Hebrews to stay in Egypt at the very moment when standing with loins girt and staffs in hand, they have been invited by God to flee from its servitude and to meet him in the promised Land. St. John Damascene protested long ago against such imaginings in a text that the catechism of the Council of Trent echoed for the sake of pastors: "It is not," said the great doctor of the eighth century, "that the body of the Lord which went up to heaven at the Ascension now descends from heaven, it is rather that the bread and wine are transformed into the body and blood of Christ."[1] The same catechism, echoing in turn one of the most liberal teachings of St. Thomas, positively invites pastors to "teach that Christ is not in the sacrament as in a place."[2] Such teachings are the only ones that do not cause rational difficulties too complex to handle, but primarily, and more profoundly, are the only ones that respect the basic orientation of the eucharistic Pasch.

One who has begun to glimpse in the paschal perspective of its revelation the breadth and reality of this mystery does not react first and foremost in the direction of situating it in this world order once more; this could never be. Nor is one inclined to consider it in any static way, but on the contrary, to lend oneself to it in adoration and in an active communion of love in that irresistible attraction, translation, or recapitulation (all biblical images to be understood in a metaphysical order as we shall explain later) by which that mystery never ceases to draw along the whole Church and all of creation into those greater depths of the transcendent mystery of God. Once again, it is a question of a paschal mystery, that is, of "passing over," and hence the term of the passage, its orientation, is the new and eternal Covenant in the Holy Spirit.

Having established this basic objective or orientation of the eucharistic Pasch, we must still go over each of the intervening stages and point out the reality each time. At the same time, it will be shown to what degree this mystery is one of universal communion.

---

[1] *De Fide orthod.*, Chap. 14; quoted in the Catechism of the Council of Trent, Chap. 19.

[2] *Ibid.*, IIIa, q. 76, a. 5.

The Relevance of Transubstantiation

"This is my body, this is my blood." It all begins with the mystery of this change which takes place on the level of being and, at least in its term since the Resurrection and Ascension of Jesus, it is the substance of his body and the substance of his blood outside of our cosmic space and time. In order to express it, the magisterium of the Church has adopted the term "transubstantiation," which has ordinarily been defined thus: "The change consists in this: By the power of God the whole substance of bread is changed into the whole substance of the body of Jesus Christ, and the whole substance of the wine into the whole substance of his blood without any change on the part of Our Lord himself" (cf. Catechism of the Council of Trent, Chap. 18).

"Without any change on the part of Our Lord himself." In God's eternity, where the sacred humanity is since the Ascension, there is no change; and only a misdirected imagination would think of the body and blood of the risen Savior as being themselves affected in any way by the innumerable eucharistic consecrations accomplished in our cosmic time and space since the original Last Supper. Since its ascension into God the sacred humanity of the Savior, which shares in the glory of God, "draws all things to itself," but is not itself attracted or modified in any way by anything. Jesus entered wholly into that state of the "Father of lights in which there is neither movement nor shadow of change" (Jas. 1: 17). Placed at the summit of creation, including the material world, and assuming it wholly by his sacred humanity, alpha as well as omega (cf. Rev. 1: 8; 21: 6), end as well as beginning (cf. Rev. 21: 6), and ending as well as principle (cf. Rev. 22: 13), Jesus Christ in the glory of the Father transcends both in the end as well as in the beginning the order of change and succession which is proper to material creation.

So it is entirely on the side of the bread and wine that the mystery lies. The term of the new Pasch is immutable since it is in eternity. If there is change, then it is entirely in the starting point of this Pasch, in the bread and wine. What is the nature of this change and what new perspectives does it offer on our new eucharistic Pasch?

We have already seen the deep roots in nature and the cosmos for the material reality of the bread and wine, and we have seen how the cosmic dimension of the eucharistic mystery suggested a continuation in the Last Supper of the ancient sacrifice of Melchizedek that might be called "naturalistic." At this point, let us enter into the perspective and follow the original action of the new Pasch, as we continue it beyond the cosmos where it meets the mystery of Christ. What really happens when Christ, pronouncing over the bread of our soil and the wine of our vineyards the words of consecration, affirms that these beautiful fruits of our land are his body and his blood? It is clear that here also the physical elements of bread and wine *do not become* the physical elements of the body and blood of Jesus. Between these two there is no proportion; no relationship of the physical order is established that belongs to space and time. The Lord does not say that the bread and wine *become* his body and blood, he affirms that they *are* just that. It is on the level of being, not of physical appearances which alone lend themselves to becoming, that they are the body and blood of the Lord. In the entire realm of physical appearances, they remain what they were: same size, same color, same chemical composition when analyzed, same capacity for corruption and transformation. But all this, we repeat, in no way concerns the body and blood of the Savior which in their glorified state are henceforth in another realm. If, however, the bread and wine *are* the body and blood, it is because they possess, besides the physical elements by which they belong, and always will belong, to this universe of space and time, another principle of being that does not stem from this physical universe. It is in the order of that other principle of being that the transference, the "passing over" affirmed in our Lord's words, occurs: This *is* my body, This *is* my blood.

That principle of being according to the common teaching of the Church is called substance. A transubstantiation has taken place. There are important reasons for definitely avoiding when speaking to the faithful to whom the Word of God is addressed the scholarly analyses of theologians and especially the discussions of the Scholastics. However, it is also important to secure for them the benefit of this common teaching to a point. To express the marvels of the Eucharist, the terms "substance" and "transubstantiation" have to be used, it seems.

At this point, we have established that the substance of bread and the substance of wine is a principle, not one which is physical in the sense of physics as the science of the changing realities of the cosmos, but a metaphysical principle in the sense that metaphysics considers the being, as such, of all reality. This principle of being, called substance, we define as that which sustains in being, in existence, the bread and the wine and all their physical aspects. Pushing the analysis further we note that this substance presents three aspects. According to the first, which is certainly the most basic, it is something which holds itself in being, unlike physical appearances, which from the point of view of being, hold themselves in being by means of substance. The round shape, the whiteness, or the chemical composition of the host do not exist in themselves but in the host considered as substance. If the substance of the host gives existence to this circular shape, chemical composition, or whiteness, it is, first of all, because it exists itself. Thus, substance is primarily that which holds itself in existence by itself.

Second, substance seems to be precisely that which allows the appearances to exist, to hold themselves in being. To the existence of the substance of bread the appearances owe their own proper existence, but inversely the substance of the bread is the support in existence of the physical appearances of the latter. There is something real here even if the reality referred to concerns the physical appearances which are in relation to substance called accidents.

Third, substance, at least in its material realities, seems to be qualified itself by the appearances or accidents that it sustains in being. The substance of the bread exists only as round, white, and composed of chemical elements. But obviously—and this is important for the eucharistic mystery—this third aspect of substance belongs only to material substance and more especially to such as exist in our universe of space and time.

Having made this analysis, what is its consequence for our study of the eucharistic mystery? We already hold as certain that the body of Christ since his Ascension no longer belongs to our universe of space and time, but to that order of eternity where "he is seated at the right hand of the Father." He cannot therefore be affected in any way by the physical appearances of bread and wine in accord with the third aspect of substance outlined above. Moreover, even at the Last Supper it was not in the order of physical appearances that the Savior through his emphasis on being had situated the mystery of the eucharistic Pasch. The facts themselves confirm this. Although he still belonged to our cosmic universe, his body had not obviously undergone any change in this order as a consequence of the words of consecration. Clearly, it is because the physical and cosmic order as such does not enter into the mystery although, as we shall see later, it produces it.

We hold that by the act of transubstantiation the body and blood of Jesus, the term of the change brought about, do not become the subject in which the physical appearance or accidents of bread and wine inhere although deprived of their own substance. Since it does not not belong to this universe of space and time where the consecrated bread and wine belong as far as concerns the physico-chemical qualities that we call appearances or species, the substance of the body and the blood cannot become the term of any transformation of these qualities. We can see that such a transformation does not take place. That is what the Scholastic theologians insist upon when they deny that after the consecration the species or accidents of the bread and wine "inhere" as such in the substance of the body and blood of the Savior and when they appeal thereafter to divine omnipotence to explain how the eucharistic accidents, physically considered, fail to inhere in any substance after the consecration. Moreover, the insistence on this point of certain theologians can lead one to think that they do not define substance with sufficient distinctness as a metaphysical principle, at the outset as St. Thomas, on the other hand, invites them to do in his teaching.

However this may be, according to the last of these three ways of looking at substance, one must conclude that it is not in the physical order, nor, for that matter, anywhere within the universe of space and time that transubstantiation takes place.

This precise distinction has a great bearing on the paschal mystery. This is true not only because it would be otherwise unthinkable: How could the body and blood of Christ be intrinsically the term of hypothetical physico-chemical changes produced by countless consecrations of our hosts and chalices? It is also and more profoundly because in this eucharistic mystery, as in any other mystery, our cosmic universe, considered in the physical aspects which it now has, cannot enter the kingdom of God. "...and those who deal with the world as though they had no dealings with it. For the form of this world is passing away" (1 Cor. 7: 31; cf. also Ps. 102: 27; Is. 51: 6; 1 Jn. 2: 17). Just as the body of the glorified risen Christ, while remaining a body and not a spirit (Lk. 24: 38) is in a different condition from the one that was his before his death, in the same way our cosmic universe will have to disappear in its death in the latter days before giving place to "the new heavens and the new earth" (2 Pet. 3: 13). We are as ignorant of the nature of that world as we are of the nature of glorified bodies. In each case we know only that there is a break between the two conditions of material creation which in itself would suffice to assure us that by its origin the mystery of the Pasch and of transubstantiation is not, and cannot be, located within the physical order. Considered in their physical elements, the bread and wine of our eucharistic Pasch are called to disappear as everything in this world once they have fulfilled their marvelous role in this universe where matter itself has the task of leading men to "pass over" toward God.

The results of the inquiry just made must not incline us to mistake or minimize the relevance in its cosmic origins of the eucharistic Pasch. The fact that in the normal course of things in the universe, physical appearances inhere in substance and therefore qualify it, is of completely secondary importance in the metaphysical consideration of being referred to here. From the metaphysician's point of view, the most decisive factor is that the accidents exist only by borrowing from the very existence of their substance. This substance holds the appearances in being much more profoundly than it is qualified by the accidents inhering in it as subject. This is the second of the three aspects of substances outlined above. If by hypothesis—and this is the very hypothesis that the Eucharist is going to actualize—this substance belongs to an order other than the physical and cosmic order of its accidents, to an order in which it can sustain them in being without their qualifying it in turn because they have not point of entry, then in this case substance will be the principle of existence for such accidents without being affected by them. This is what happens in the eucharistic mystery. When on leaving our cosmic universe and entering into God's eternity at the Ascension, the holy and glorified humanity of Jesus, considered as substance, that is, as an existing reality, becomes by the words of consecration the principle of existence for the bread and wine; or rather, since there is no possible development in it, one must say that henceforth, the bread and wine receive their existence from it, just as before the consecration they held their existence from their own substance. This food, while keeping its physical condition, loses its autonomy at the precise moment when the words of consecration affirm, "This is," and the bread and wine no longer subsist as the physical bread and wine, except by borrowing from the subsistence of the sacred humanity of the Savior. Inasmuch as physically these accidents do not inhere in the substance of the body and blood of the Savior, they have no other existence except that of the body and blood to which they have been transubstantiated. At the same time it must be admitted that if, in the Eucharist, "the figure of this cosmos," that is, of the physical elements, passes away as in all material things, the profound reality of the Eucharist is a principle that does not pass away. It is a principle of immortal and incorruptible subsistence, namely, the sacred and glorified humanity of Jesus "who dies no more."

He Who Eats Me Will Live by Me

From this it follows necessarily that every communion is a participation in the incorruptible existence of Jesus: "This is the bread which came down from heaven, not such as the fathers ate and died; he who eats this bread will live forever" (Jn. 6: 58). It is well known how much devotion the eucharistic tradition of the Greek Fathers had for this aspect of our mystery, actually seeing in it for our own bodies the necessarily efficacious seed of their immortality and incorruptible future. And it is quite true that by reason of the transubstantiation all consecrated hosts and any consecrated wine having no other subsistence than in the flesh and blood of the risen Savior establish communion for those who consume them with the immortal and incorruptible existence of that flesh and that blood which is in the glory of the

Father. Consequently, and most truly, even at this stage of our paschal ascent we perceive that the same Spirit who vivified the crucified body in the Resurrection is beginning to vivify our mortal bodies also (cf. Rom. 8: 11), and this is done by means of the body of the Savior communicated to us during his mortal life in the mystery of the eucharistic Pasch. Even now, by reason of the glorified condition of Christ, to whom it makes us "pass over," each communion is an ascent toward immortality.

The Cosmic Dimension of Eucharistic Reality

All this is the necessary consequence of the basic relevance of transubstantiation. Even in this first phase the marvelous character and the religious fullness of this mystery appears. Already the whole cosmic universe at numberless points of space and time seems to be centered on the existence of the sacred and glorified humanity of Christ. Indeed, whether one thinks of the remote preparation of the wheat in our hosts and the wine in our chalices, or whether one thinks of the incalculably frequent eucharistic consecrations which from the Ascension to the Parousia in all points of space and time have never ceased, they do not, and will not, cease to transubstantiate this wine and these hosts into the body and blood of that sacred humanity. The whole universe is involved. It presents for the labor and nourishment of men a convergence of aim, an orientation in process towards that sacred humanity and thereby toward God. These are countless cosmic extensions of the Incarnation, if you like, provided that they are regarded, as the Incarnation should be regarded, not as a descent of the sacred humanity into our multitudinous hosts and chalices, any more than the Word descends into the sacred humanity, but rather as an assumption of these hosts and the wine in our chalices into the glorified existence of the sacred humanity, which itself has been assumed by the eternal Person of the Word.

In this light the statements of St. Paul about the plan of God to recapitulate all things in Christ, including those on this earth (cf. Eph. 1: 10; Col. 1: 20) take on a new significance. Even in its material reality the whole universe appears as a "divine milieu" inviting human beings by its very orientation to go beyond it to God. From the fact of transubstantiation alone, this material universe, wherever there is a host or a consecrated chalice, seems to be all filled with the presence of Jesus Christ, not as some sort of indefinable presence, but as the personal presence, corporeal even, of the risen and glorified Lord, of the Lord who from then on irresistibly draws into the glory of his Father the whole of creation directed toward him.

Because of transubstantiation and because of the presence of Jesus which it brings about in the cosmic universe, a presence of attraction, this universe, even as it continues to be the desert for the People of God, a desert which must be crossed by them before entering the promised land, can no longer be a desert of solitude for them: Jesus, their leader who is their head since he is in the glory of heaven, and among them since he is in the host, never ceases to attract them heavenward and to strengthen them on the journey much more efficaciously than Yahweh in the desert of the Exodus could attract the Hebrews by the column of fire or the cloud, or strengthen them with the manna.

*The Relevance of the Paschal Communion in
Universal Love*

And yet, even here, "the flesh profiteth nothing, it is
the Spirit that quickeneth." However impressive, in their
cosmic and metaphysical basis, the reality and breadth
of the eucharistic Pasch may seem already, they will be
even more so on the level of spiritual mysteries which
the activity of this Pasch obliges us to approach. The
"flesh," in this case, is that innumerable multitude of
Eucharists extended through unending space and time,
from the original Last Supper to the Parousia. Its
existential reality is in the unique, holy, and henceforth
glorified humanity of the Lord. But this flesh is made
to be eaten. The table is set, and the wedding feast is
ready; the guests are now to sit down and eat (cf. Mt.
22: 2ff.). In the eating of this sacred flesh, they all are
going to enter into real, existential communion with the
sacred humanity of Jesus whereby they partake of the
wedding feast of the new and eternal Covenant between
God and men. The transubstantiation is for communion,
and the reality of the bread and wine has no other end
except to introduce the second.

We see now the great depth of this reality and the
wide extension of this communion. Let us begin with the
latter. The Last Supper, we saw, is viewed essentially as
a fraternal meal. Before taking the bread and wine and
before pronouncing over them the words of consecration,
the Lord started to prepare his disciples by acts and
words, the sole object of which was to intensify their
fraternal charity. We have seen that this was the immediate and indispensable preparation for the subsequent
unfolding of the new paschal mystery. It is still the law.
Just as the whole cosmic evolution and all human work

have prepared the bread and wine that are to be transubstantiated, so fraternal charity must already have begun to unite those who, by partaking of the bread and wine together, are going to be caught up into a great mystery of communion that is not only intentional but real. Here again, reality infinitely surpasses the preparations. The long process of cosmic germination of our wheat and our vines is certainly transcended when it enters by transubstantiation into the mystery of all the bread and all the wine which throughout time and space persist only in the existence of the holy humanity of Jesus. Likewise, the immense aspiration of fraternal charity among the disciples of Jesus toward unity—an aspiration which he gives them by his example—truly achieves unity in the eucharistic mystery: "Because there is one bread, we who are many are one body, for we all partake of the one bread" (1 Col. 10: 17).

Is this really what happens each time we receive communion? The preceding pages make this clear. Because of transubstantiation and the connections that exist because of it between all the hosts and all the consecrated chalices and the unique existence of the body and blood of the Savior, we all find ourselves connected with this unique existence of our head and leader. We all communicate with his unique existence. "All": that means not only the restricted group of Christians living at one time in one place but all the communicants of all times and all places, since the glorious life of the Savior transcends time and space. I truly eat the same bread that the apostles and first Christians ate. It is the same bread eaten by the martyrs of the persecutions, the countless confessors of Christianity of Byzantium or Rome, the ascetics and virgins, the saints of the past and those of yesterday, the myriads of faithful in the old

Christian countries or missionary Christians on the way towards the future, and finally the incalculable throng of communicants who from now until the Parousia will never stop partaking of it.

We have all been, are, and shall be seated at the same unique banquet. The consecrations that lead to this may be innumerable, the liturgies in the variety of their human splendor that prepare them may succeed in bringing them to the wedding feast, but in the last analysis, these always lead to the one and only existence of the glorified Christ in which all hearts are united in unity. Just as the initiative for this immense ascending movement of the Church towards its Lord comes not so much from those who enter into it as from the Lord himself who draws them, so it must be admitted through the mystery of the eucharistic Pasch, keystone and crown of the whole sacramental order, that the risen Lord effects the unification and recapitulation in himself of his whole Church mentioned by the apostle, Paul (cf. Eph. 1: 10). Rather than a petition, the admirable eucharistic prayer of the *Didache* which follows is primarily an act of faith shot through with eschatological hopes: "Just as the broken bread was first sowed on the hills, then harvested and made into one, so thy Church gathers together from the ends of the earth into thy kingdom, because thine is the power and the glory through Jesus Christ forever and ever" (Did. 9: 4). Individual communions should be seen in this, the only true context.

And yet, we are still only at the threshold of the mystery of unity which the eucharistic Pasch brings about in those who yield to its action. If our unity is based only on the original truth, that is, on transubstantiation, which allows all the communicants to be nourished

by the one and only existence of the Savior's body and
blood, then it would last in each one only for the few
moments during which the consecrated bread and wine
maintain in him the real presence of the body and blood.
When finished with the outward banquet, each one
would relapse into solitude. Its dispersion would take
away from the unity. This may be the case. The communicant, after reaching that point, may withdraw from
the paschal movement. But if, on the other hand, he
lends himself docilely to this movement, he will inevitably
be led onward into the mystery of the new and eternal
Covenant where the definitive and unbreakable unity is
to be consummated and sealed. "He who eats me," says
Jesus, "will live because of me" (Jn. 6: 57). Following
the direction of this paschal relevance, what will this life
be like for the communicant, and how will it make him
progress towards that mystery of unity which through
the relevance of transubstantiation and communion began to be established in him with the Lord and with all
the members of the body of the Lord, which is the
Church? This amounts to asking what the paschal immolation contributes to the real mystery of unity that
Pasch brings about.

The Truth of the Paschal Sacrifice

"He who eats me will live by me" (Jn. 6: 57). In
what direction does Jesus influence those who receive him
in the eucharistic Pasch? In the new Pasch, the immense
fraternal meal in which all the members of the messianic
people partake of the same bread precedes the paschal
immolation and introduces it. The path leads from the
supper room to Calvary. The words of the Lord are not

only, "This is my body," "This is my blood," but also "This is my body which is delivered over for you" (Lk. 22: 19; cf. also Jn. 6: 51), "This is my blood, the blood of the Covenant, shed for a great number for the forgiveness of sins" (Mt. 26: 28; cf. also Mk. 14: 22). As we have seen, everything in the institution of the Eucharist—the words and rites—manifests the close link between the Last Supper and the Passion. "For as often as you eat this bread and drink the cup, you proclaim the Lord's death until he comes" (1 Cor. 11: 26).

And thus, if it is true because of the reality of transubstantiation that by the glorified humanity of Jesus the only humanity which really exists, all Eucharists are connected with the infinite multitude of the Church's members who partake of these Eucharists (even as at the Last Supper the disciples were closely attached by their first communion with the existence of his mortal humanity, and just as each consecration celebrated during the triduum of his death would have attached them to the existence of the divine body), it is also true that by its symbolic mode, or more precisely its sacramental mode, each Eucharist in whatever situation is connected with the Passion. At the end of the first Eucharist, the Last Supper, Jesus had invited his disciples to accompany him to the Garden of Olives and beyond, and we saw that they scarcely had the strength to follow him. Likewise, if someone had consecrated between the death of Jesus and his Resurrection, this consecration would have been connected with the victory of Christ and would have won all those who would have been nourished by it. But first of all, it would unite them with the Passion. Since Christ is now glorified, every communion effectively tends to unite those who communicate with the glory of their head, first by leading them through his victory, that is, through his Passion and cross. Every communion, St. Thomas explains, unites us with "Christus passus," meaning, with Christ glorified, whom we receive in an unglorified state. We discover this in the sacrificial rites of the Last Supper and our Masses, but in an immolating state.

This is also important. If by the eucharistic Pasch, the immense multitude of the People of God is really drawn into the victorious strength of the risen Christ which the Eucharist gives us in communion into the way of the Passion and cross that Jesus took when he left the Cenacle, and if this prodigious way of the cross, again because of the relevance of this communion, receives its direction and draws all its strength from this same victory of Christ crucified, then it follows because of the Eucharist, that the immense spiritual struggles of this people and the crushing burden of sufferings that they endure on the way to God are in close and real continuity with the suffering and struggle of Jesus on Calvary.

By the Eucharist, the whole Church, enlarged by the fraternal meal of the Supper to the universal dimensions of all humanity, receives the power of offering after Christ all the sufferings of men of goodwill. This immense sacrifice of the Church is seen as an extension of Christ's sacrifice, or rather as making one with him, in the one and only paschal mystery, all the virtue and all the efficacity of the Church's sacrifice because in the paschal mystery is only the extension of Christ's. Just as Christ's sacrifice had the redemption of the world as its immediate end and first result, the Church's sacrifice, which continues his work, extends the redemption of the world by the same unique power. All communicants of all times and all places—the virgins, the confessors, the ascetics and martyrs, the faithful and bishops, the apostles and doctors—were taught by the action of the new Pasch, into which they were drawn by their communions to "rejoice in my sufferings for your sake, and in my flesh I complete what is lacking in Christ's afflictions for the sake of his body, that is, the church" (Col. 1: 24), or else to "lay down our lives for the brethren" (1 Jn. 3: 16). All have generously allowed themselves to be carried along in the movement of the new Pasch and all have accepted the duty of continuing their fraternal meal in an active effort to redeem the world in union with the Passion of the Lord, the only effective way to redemption. Even the act of extending their fraternal charity to all people of good will can be something to offer to the Lord as a continuation of his redemptive Passion and include even the trials and sufferings of men that may seem far from him.

But here again, because of the relevance of the eucharistic Pasch, one should see that the initiative in this great sacrifice of the Church that gives value to every human suffering by placing it through the Eucharist in the wake of Christ's Passion comes from the Lord himself. When the disciples had not yet received strength from the risen Lord, they said after the Last Supper that they would follow Jesus everywhere and die with him, but because of their weakness they did not as Jesus had warned them (Mt. 26: 31-35). But when Jesus had won his victory, it became theirs, and from then on, they who were incapable of following him during his Passion became, as Peter, capable of following him later (cf. Jn. 13: 36). But then it was because another girded them and led them where they themselves would never have been able to, nor have chosen, to go (cf. Jn. 21: 18-19). The baptism of blood, with which he himself was to be baptized, was theirs also, and for the same reasons, but after him and by virtue of this first baptism (cf. Mk. 10: 39).

In brief, it is Jesus who is the priest of this unique sacrifice insofar as the strength exercised and the reasons for it are his, but in return, all the sufferings of men, from the witness of blood given before the whole universe to the most hidden act of renunciation, if accepted with redemptive intent, in the eucharistic continuation of the Lord's Passion, begin to be taken up by him into his own unique sacrifice and to have a redemptive value. One is reminded of the "pure offerings" of the messianic prophet Malachi: "Great is the Lord, beyond the border of Israel ... For from the rising of the sun to its setting my name is great among the nations, and in every place incense is offered to my name, and a pure offering; for my name is great among the nations, says the Lord of hosts" (Mal. 1: 5, 11). Just as the multitude of hosts and of consecrated chalices are taken up by transubstantiation into the unique existence of the sacred humanity of Christ, so also all those participating in this one immense eucharistic table can now enter, because of the unique existence in which they communicated, into a mystery of unity still to be accomplished; and even now, the action of the Pasch moving towards this consummate union, gathers up, in the unique redemptive offering of the Savior on Calvary, all the countless offerings and sacrifices that this Pasch inspires or simply finds in men of goodwill. By the Eucharist, the whole Church is drawn by Jesus into the mystery of his immolation. By the Eucharist, all the sufferings of men of goodwill take on the meaning and value of Christ's suffering.

Finally, this means that the sufferings of men receive

their inspiration from the only perfect suffering, which is that of Jesus Christ, and they thereby communicate in the mystery of the charity of Calvary which is the mystery of the new and eternal Covenant in the Holy Spirit. By this mystery everything reaches a consummation and for this mystery everything else is a preparation. And yet here below we can scarcely refer to it without diminishing it.

The Pasch of Jesus, we saw, was directed entirely toward that act of charity on the cross in which he received not only for himself but for the whole Church, the plenitude of the Holy Spirit, that is, a participation in the mysteries of God. By this act, the new and eternal Covenant was consummated. Towards this act, the eucharistic Pasch is also directed according to the essential aspects of the fraternal meal and redemptive sacrifice. But there is this difference: Since this act was posited once and for all on Calvary and since the Covenant was sealed by virtue of this act and also because of the relevance of this Covenant, the Church in turn enters into it by its offerings and its consecrations. It is not only Jesus who draws all things to himself; it is, first, the Father who draws all things to Jesus (cf. Jn. 6: 44). Both are one and the same and are done *in* the Holy Spirit. Consequently, we notice this first in Jesus himself. The action of the Pasch and the entering into possession of the goods of the Covenant coincide. The whole dynamism of fraternal charity in the paschal meal as the whole paschal and redemptive immolation in which this charity must be continued is not tending towards the future establishment of the mystery of unity, they are already in this mystery; they *are* already this mystery and receive their efficacy from it. Some tension persists of course, but it is only the eschatological tension of the mysteries in progress toward their consummation. Just as truly as every consecrated host contains the body and blood of Jesus, every act of self-sacrifice already includes the Holy Spirit. By the Eucharist, Jesus communicates himself fully to those who follow him, that is, to those whom he brings into the paschal mystery where he first received it for them in its plenitude.

Hence it is one and the same Spirit who in the eucharistic Pasch truly animates the whole body of Christ, uniting the head with the members and the members with one another in a living unity the reality of which is none other than the reality of the mystery of the Holy Spirit in God. Since by transubstantiation the whole multitude of the People of God has become one body in Christ so that they are members of each other (cf. Rom. 12: 4; 1 Cor. 12: 12ff.), and since by reason of the fraternal charity that leads them into the redemptive action of the Pasch, this multitude from now on has only one Spirit, at which they "drink," says St. Paul (1 Cor. 12: 12), the Holy Spirit of God. *"By* Jesus," the apostle says elsewhere in one of his trinitarian formulas, "we have each and all access *to* the Father in the *same* Spirit" (Eph. 2: 18). And lastly: "There is one body and one Spirit, just as you were called to the one hope that belongs to your call, one Lord, one faith, one baptism, one God and Father of us all, who is above all and through all and in all" (Eph. 4: 4-6).

We must here recall the immense recapitulation of the entire universe by means of transubstantiation toward the holy and glorious humanity of Jesus at the right hand of the Father, and we must crown it with the active presence in this mystery of the Holy Spirit of God who is the Spirit of charity and unity. "Because the

Spirit of the Lord has filled the world" (Wis. 1: 7), the Church sings on the feast of Pentecost, the climax of the paschal cycle. Indeed through the eucharistic Pasch, the Spirit is made present in the universe and in the People of God who make their way to heaven in a more extensive way than the inspired author of the book of Wisdom could have imagined.

Thus it is in and through the Holy Spirit, by means of the eucharistic Pasch, that the recapitulation and unification of all the People of God is consummated, and all things are brought together in the mystery of Christ.

Conclusion

On reaching the end of these pages, the author is the first to realize their imperfection. Although the general idea is expressed with sufficient clarity, and some light shed on the subject in question, many aspects that were only touched upon could well be discussed in greater detail, clarified, and emphasized.

One would hope at least to have furthered the two points mentioned at the beginning, the first being a better understanding by the faithful of the great eucharistic mystery, especially the immense communitarian and cosmic perspectives that are essential to it. The progressive exposition of this mystery in successive stages has shown how contrary to its essentials it is to consider it purely from an individualistic point of view and to focus attention only on those who participate in it. Its whole meaning is directed toward the recapitulation in heaven of all things in the mystery of Christ and ultimately in the mystery of the God of love.

It is hoped also that the cause of pastoral theology and theology plain and simple has been served in the attempt to remain close to the concrete economy of salvation and accessible in its approach to the minds of the People of God. The author has tried to remain faithful in his conclusions to this level of the economy of salvation which is the center of interest not only for pastoral theology but also for the liturgy. It should consequently enrich them both.

It is a method of pastoral teaching that is based on the concrete economy in which revelation is providentially unfolded. In this economy are found not only trains of thought that are divinely guaranteed and that deepen the content of this same revelation but, since they deal with the mystery of the last days, an invitation as well to see beyond the historical and concrete order of this economy to the transcendent level of theology.

Finally, it should be said that this work is dependent not upon purely speculative and abstract thought but on the historical circumstances in which God in his providential and human economy chose to reveal and communicate his mysteries to his people.